ALSO BY TORI SPELLING

celebraTORI

Presenting . . . Tallulah

uncharted terriTORI

Mommywood

sTORI telling

SPELLING
It Like It Is

TORI SPELLING

WITH HILARY LIFTIN

GALLERY BOOKS

NEW YORK LONDON TORONTO SYDNEY NEW DELHI

GALLERY BOOKS

NEW YORK LONDON TORONTO SYDNEY NEW DELHI

G

Gallery Books
A Division of Simon & Schuster, Inc.
1230 Avenue of the Americas
New York, NY 10020

First Gallery Books hardcover edition October 2013

GALLERY BOOKS and colophon are registered trademarks of Simon & Schuster, Inc.

For information about special discounts for bulk purchases, please contact Simon & Schuster Special Sales at 1-866-506-1949 or business@simonandschuster.com.

The Simon & Schuster Speakers Bureau can bring authors to your live event. For more information or to book an event, contact the Simon & Schuster Speakers Bureau at 1-866-248-3049 or visit our website at www.simonspeakers.com.

Interior design by Davina Mock-Maniscalco

Manufactured in the United States of America

10   9   8   7   6   5   4   3   2   1

Library of Congress Cataloging-in-Publication data is available.

ISBN 978-1-4516-2859-3
ISBN 978-1-4516-2864-7 (ebook)

To my complete family—
Dean, Jack, Liam, Stella, Hattie, and Finn

And . . .
Coco
Mitzi
Minnie
Ferris
Chiquita
Missy Snuggles
Phyllis
Maxine
Rosie
Princess
Sully
Benny
Cinnamon
Oreo
Trix
Hank
Totes
Juliet
Large Marge
Jackson
Phyllis Diller
Sugarplum
Ginger
Blueberry Fish
Raspberry Fish

Contents

INTRODUCTION:
Living a Lie

The cover of *Star* magazine said, "Tori's Lies Exposed." Ooh. What could it be this time? Was I cheating on my husband with someone who looked exactly like him? Had I been switched at birth with the true non-heir to the Spelling fortune?

But no. When I opened the magazine all I found was just a rehash of *Star*'s favorite story: Dean and I were breaking up. He was about to walk out on me. Blah, blah, blah. Heard it all before. It's a story they've written so many times that I'm pretty sure their article list is on an annual cycle. If it's March, Dean and I must be on the rocks.

Not to judge, but I can't help feeling like the decent, moral, cream-of-the-crop journalists at *Star* magazine aren't earning their keep. If you're going to lie, lay it on us! Go big. Make up something good and juicy. Disclose that our chicken Coco is actually Paris Hilton's stolen poodle in disguise. Or that Chelsea Handler has been right all these years: I am actually a man. (These are examples of creative lying, *Star*, and you can have them for free. Be my guest.)

There was no substance to the article. An insider was quoted as saying, "She always goes on and on about how strong their marriage is, but the truth is that it's all totally fake—her marriage is a sham." The article said that I'd kicked Dean out. He'd packed his bags. The accompanying photo on the front cover was of Dean carrying two shopping bags. One of them was from a children's clothing store. If you looked closely, you could see where I'd been cropped out of the picture. A bit of my leg was next to his. I recognized our outfits and where we were. That was me and my husband, Christmas shopping for our children. Way to go, *Star*, you got us.

It's funny (and annoying) to read that my love for Dean is a lie. My love for Dean is very real. Like everyone else we have our strengths and weaknesses, our ups and downs. That's what real love is. I'm thick skinned, though. Must be all the scar tissue from the plastic surgeries *Star* thinks I've had. The stories don't really get under my skin. But the story *Star* missed (surprise, surprise) is that I've lived my life in public on a reality show for six years, and with any public life come manipulations, exaggerations, and, well, realities behind the edited version of that life. I hate to give *Star* any attention for their feeble attempt at capturing my life. But my reality show, *Tori & Dean,* is over after six seasons on Oxygen. It's a perfect time to go behind the scenes the way poor *Star* never could and fill in some of the missing pieces.

IT'S BEEN AN especially challenging couple of years. On *Tori & Dean* we moved houses constantly. At first, to me and Dean, my recurring need to move seemed driven by changes in our family. We needed more space because our stepson was moving back from Canada. Then we were having another baby. Then our house felt too big for us, and we wanted more land for our animals. And I won-dered if I was subconsciously looking for another design project. Those were our reasons for moving, and that's what we said on the show. But as my real estate obsession persists, it's starting to look more compulsive. Moving is expensive, and I've put us in a precarious financial situa-tion. I'm no stranger to that, but usually I drum up some work and correct our course. This time, when I should have been working, I was flat on my back in a hospital bed, and we dug ourselves deeper into the hole.

Tori & Dean showed us fighting and then renewing our vows, but it didn't tell the full story of Dean's and my ups and downs. There's a reality behind that reality. I want to share our hardest period, and the real moment I fell in love with my husband all over again.

People know that our fourth child, Finn, came right on the heels of our third, and the press showed cute pictures of my pregnancy bump and the "look how quickly she slimmed down" after-pictures. I talked in the press about my health issues surrounding the pregnancy, but nobody really knows the impact it had on me and my family.

Our family is complete now: me; Dean; our four beloved children; my stepson, Jack; and a somewhat changing menagerie of pets and farm animals. The show that tracked our family is over, but we go on changing (houses), growing (our suburban farm), and getting into unexpected scrapes (paparazzi-fleeing car accidents). I'm the first to admit that I haven't figured things out yet. But at least I tell it like it is.

The Test Is Conclusive

The first sign that something wasn't exactly normal happened in the middle of work craziness. On Thursday, February 10, 2011, in the middle of doing photo shoots for my about-to-be-published party-planning book, *celebraTORI*, my gay husband (whom I call my "gusband") Mehran and I were scheduled to fly to Tampa. I had an appearance on the Home Shopping Network (HSN) to promote our jewelry line. I had started freaking out about the plane trip a week in advance. (That part was completely normal.)

Every guest who appears on HSN to sell their products agrees to do a middle-of-the-night segment—to pay your dues. Then you appear again on a prime-time block the following day. It's a brutal schedule on a normal day—I'm sure Suzanne Somers and George Foreman didn't relish hawking their goods in the dead of night—and my fear of flying compounded the stress, but as I was soon to find out, this wasn't a normal day. Mehran and I left L.A. in the morning, transferred in Dallas, and arrived in Tampa around dinnertime. I went on the air at two in the morning. The next day, after meetings with HSN, I was back on the air from four to six P.M.

By the time I got to my prime-time slot, I was exhausted and a little bit nauseated. Story of my life. I'd come directly to HSN from working on *celebraTORI*. I created and threw four parties for the book, coming up with everything from invitations to favors. For the photo shoots, I was involved in everything: art direction, props, food styling, and fluffer to Coco, our white silkie bearded chicken. I had plenty of people to help me, but because I'm incapable of delegating anything beyond lawn care (although I do like the grass to be mowed to 2.5 inches), I styled and directed each image. I blinked my eyes—and now I was on the air.

What I said about our jewelry wasn't scripted. With a perky smile glued on my face, I talked about how my pieces were "vintage-inspired with a modern twist" and added, "I call it 'modage.'" The producer was in my earpiece, giving me merchandising updates: "We have a hundred more of this necklace. We're almost sold out of the coral bracelet."

Everything was going swimmingly until . . . I started to feel sick to my stomach, like I might throw up. There was no stopping the HSN train. I was on the air, live. At home, people were watching me, looking at the jewels Mehran and I had worked so hard to design, calling to talk with me, and waiting to decide if today they would make a purchase. The sales ticker was within sight, and the speed at which its numbers rolled higher was an immediate reflection of how good a job I was doing. So, sickness be damned, on I went.

"I used to make this particular piece for high-end boutiques in New York. It was worn by celebrities. Now you can look like a million bucks, but you don't have to spend it!" Ooh. I could see that the TV viewers at home loved that one. All of a sudden they were picking up the phone. The sales numbers started to run up higher and higher. I glanced off to the side stage, where Mehran was standing. There was a big clock near him, showing me how many minutes I had left. Twenty minutes to go. *I'm going to throw up. What if I throw up on the air? I'll never live it down.* The Soup *embarrassing clip of the week, here I come.*

Every so often there was a sixty-second commercial break. Hidden from the camera, I had the Diet Dr Pepper with a straw (so I didn't ruin my lips) that had become my HSN tradition and good-luck charm. I would sip from it while the host touched up her lipstick. Usually I glanced at Mehran to see how our sales were going. This time I mouthed to him, "I'm so sick. I'm not going to make it." Unfortunately, this too fell into the category of normal. I'm always sick.

Mehran mouthed back, "Me too," and rolled his eyes. Much as Mehran had in the past taken on my baby weight, he also has sympathetic headaches, stomach problems, and low energy. I know we're BFFs, but even my ailments aren't my own anymore. When he has a headache, I'm like, "Please, can you be a little more original? Maybe a kidney stone?"

And . . . we were back on the air. "The best thing my customers say to me is, 'I bought this necklace for myself, but my daughter wanted to borrow it. Then my granddaughter.' I make timeless pieces." (*Check out this bracelet. I'm about to vomit all over it. Your granddaughter would love the very same one!*)

This wasn't exactly Broadway, but the show had to go on. Story of my life. I sold my jewelry with a smile, counting down the minutes. As soon as we wrapped, I turned to the host.

"So great to be here," I said. "Loved it. See you next time." I gave the host a big hug good-bye. I walked off the stage as gracefully as I could in my high heels; ran through my dressing room, where HSN's jewelry buyers were sitting on couches, waiting to go through next season's collection with me; went into the adjoining bathroom; and promptly threw up. I had been closer than I even realized to tossing my cookies live on national TV. It would have made for some good reality TV, but the drama was wasted on real life.

Mehran went out to the HSN buyers and explained to them that I was too sick to meet. But I wiped my mouth, washed my hands, walked out, apologized, and did the meeting, sick as a dog. I spent the plane ride home in the bathroom of first class, kneeling on a paper towel, throwing up. It's the only way to fly.

OKAY, SO I figured it was food poisoning from the plane, a stomach bug, or that I was simply extremely overworked and exhausted. I got back to L.A. late that night. When I got off the plane, texts from James, an art director I'd met during the first season of *Tori & Dean* who had become my good friend and was working with me on the parties for the book, started rolling in. This time they were photos of a do-it-yourself bar, set up with vodka, champagne, soda, cassis, elderflower syrup, pomegranate syrup, and other options in glass carafes, with homemade tags hung from twine. He'd captured what I wanted, but I wished I were there.

The next day, I woke up still feeling sick. I was supposed to go straight to a photo studio, where we were working on shots for *celebraTORI*. (Even though we shot four full parties, afterward we spent full days in the studio shooting detail shots of the invitations, flowers, extra food, and other party elements in order to get the perfect lighting.) I headed to the studio, with Coco in the passenger seat—she would appear in lots of the photos as the mascot of the book. I wanted to fiddle with every detail, but after I'd driven halfway to the studio, I pulled over on the side of the road. I texted James: "*i'm dizzy. i'm going to throw up. turning around. SO sorry.*"

I felt terrible about missing the photo shoot. We were on a tight shooting schedule. We couldn't miss a day. They'd already had to do a full day of shooting while I was at HSN. There was so much to be done, and I'm a control freak. If I wasn't there, how would I get the shots I wanted? The next day was Saturday. We were headed to Joshua Tree for the weekend. I was hosting a Cowboys and Lace party for *celebraTORI*. Of course I couldn't have it in my house. It *had* to be in the desert. Because the pictures would be that much more fabulous. I needed vintage duds for the shoot, and I didn't want my outing to be wasted, so on the way home I stopped at Jet Rag, a used-clothing store on La Brea. Coco and I ran in and grabbed a few frocks—Gunne Sax–style floral and lace prairie dresses—for the shoot in fifteen minutes flat. By the time I hurled my bag into the back of the car, I was sweating and about to puke, but it had been an amazingly productive detour. I headed home.

What happened next really should have clued me in. On the way to my house, as if on autopilot, I pulled over at a Taco Bell. I still felt sick, but I also felt a sudden and very strong desire for a number one combo: a Burrito Supreme and a Taco Supreme. And a cherry limeade. With my delicious meal in my lap, I started to drive away from the restaurant—I was fully planning to eat at home—but, oddly, I found myself parallel-parking on Ventura Boulevard. I opened the bag and wolfed the burrito and taco down. I tossed a few pieces of shredded lettuce to Coco, saying, "Sorry, that's all you get. Mama's starving." Yeah, I should have known something was up.

THE NEXT DAY I went to Joshua Tree. Dean and I had just finished shooting the last episode of *sTORIbook Weddings*. I'd begun work on the party-planning book before we finished the weddings. And Dean was staying home from Joshua Tree to get our new store, InvenTORI, ready for opening on Monday, Valentine's Day. There was a lot going on. No wonder I was sick.

We got beautiful photos of the party in the desert, but it wasn't much of a party. We'd had Game Night and Spa Day parties, both at my house, both real parties with my friends. But Cowboys and Lace was not a party at all. The Guncles, Bill and Scout, and their infant daughter, Simone, drove all the way to the desert. The show put them up at a hotel. A producer brought them to the set. There was no chitchat or festivity. It was all, "Places, everybody. We're losing the sun." At some point I said, "Oh my God, all my party guests are always gays and girls." So Vidas, the straight producer who had once buried my underwear at the demand of my psychic, Mama Lola, stepped forward, put a cowboy hat on, and joined the photo.

On the way home from the desert I shopped for InvenTORI at a fantastic antique store. There were so many great pieces that I ended up renting a U-Haul to bring it all back to L.A. We got home around eight P.M. Twelve hours later Dean and I were at InvenTORI, scrambling to make sure everything was ready to go when the doors opened at nine A.M.

The store was a madhouse. The line to enter stretched around the corner. The paparazzi were having a field day. I chatted with every single person who came in, pointing out the antique French country farm table that I'd had in every apartment and house I'd lived in since I was twenty, or a bar cart I'd found at a flea market and had enjoyed in our dining room. Coco, who was a fan fave, had to be at the store opening. We had faux-Coco fuzzy stuffed chickens made by Jellycat for sale, displayed in a chicken-wire armoire. We were shooting the sixth season of *Tori & Dean: Home Sweet Hollywood*, so our two cameramen and all our producers were there, catching the day on film.

At four in the afternoon, as I sat in our back office, everything spinning and my makeup artist Brandy giving me sips of ginger ale, I admitted defeat. Dean would have to cover for me until closing time. We didn't want to say I was sick on *Tori & Dean*—it wasn't worth dwelling on a stomach bug because nobody thought it was leading to a real story line. Instead, we said that I was going home to take care of Stella, who was sick. It was true, Stella was also actually sick, but the real reason I left was that I couldn't stand up for another minute.

I went home and climbed into bed. I was texting with Mehran, who, when he found out I wasn't feeling well, wrote *"is there anything I can bring you?"*

I wrote *"a pregnancy test?"* I knew I could trust Mehran to be discreet. I took pregnancy tests all the time. Since Dean and I always knew we wanted a third, we'd left it up to fate and hadn't used birth control in the three years since Stella was born. Whenever I felt the least bit off, I self-diagnosed myself as pregnant. I was single-handedly keeping EPT in business.

"are you serious?" he texted back.

"maybs"

In a short while, Mehran arrived with a couple pee-on-a-stick pregnancy tests. Before I pulled them out, I said, "Did you get the jenky ones with the pluses and minuses where you can't tell if you're pregnant?"

"I'm not sure. I got the most expensive ones . . ."

I pulled out the tests. Sure enough, it was the kind where if one pink line shows up in the little window, you're not pregnant, and if two lines appear, you are.

I said, "Oh no. I can't trust these. I need the ones that say 'pregnant' or 'not pregnant'!" Mehran looked embarrassed. Poor Mehi, oblivious to the subtleties and whims of a possibly pregnant woman in desperate need of a test that complies with her OCD requirements and speaks to her in the English language.

I took the test. There was one pink line. Definitely. And next to it was something else. A pink shadow? A pink cloud? The ghost of a pink line? I showed the test to Mehran.

"So?" I said, showing him the stick.

He peered at it. "Oh yeah," he said. "I can't tell."

"It's inconclusive," I said.

I drank a glass of water and took the second test into the bathroom with me. At least the tests were consistent—the results were equally vague.

Mehran concurred. "It's very inconclusive."

Now what? I was inconclusively pregnant. Or inconclusively not pregnant. Should I mention any of this to my husband, who was still at InvenTORI, selling the last of the white chicken Jellycats? (They were an unexpectedly hot item. We sold forty stuffed chickens that day.) It seemed like I'd been sick for two years, always with my migraines and weak stomach. I was the girl who cried wolf. Heck, I'd been nauseated for two weeks, and it had never even crossed Dean's mind that I might be pregnant. Never even suspected. This was a great opportunity. If I was in fact pregnant, I could surprise Dean with the news. I decided not to mention the pregnancy tests to Dean. They were inconclusive, after all.

THE NEXT DAY my assistant Dana was dropping me off at Universal to meet up with James. We were picking out rental furniture for Cocktails and Caftans, the next party I was throwing for my party-planning book. At this point only Mehran knew about my inconclusive pregnancy, and I wanted to keep it that way. I just needed to take another test—the one that spoke to me in English—and en route to Universal was my best opportunity. I just had to know. I said to Dana, "Can you do me a favor? Don't ask questions, just pull over at Walgreens."

Dana complied. I went into Walgreens, thinking I'd buy a pregnancy test and take it in their bathroom. But the minute I went in, a Walgreens staffer ran up to me.

"Tori!" she exclaimed. "I love your show." I thanked her and posed for a picture with her. I'd been seen. If I bought a pregnancy test now, it could easily be in the tabloids by morning. I walked back to the car empty-handed.

I said, "Can I ask you to do something for me that's really personal?"

Dana replied, "I've had to spoon your shit into a container to take to a doctor. Nothing's too personal." It was true. When I had stomach problems, I'd had to leave a specimen for my doctor. It had to sit in one liquid for a certain number of hours, and then it had to be transferred to another container. When Dana called the doctor about delivery, they asked if this had been done. I'd forgotten to do the transfer and I was already on set for the day. It had to be done, and for that Dana should win the Hollywood Assistant Lifetime Achievement Award for Most Disgusting Act in the Line of Duty.

"I think I'm pregnant," I said. Now there were two

people who knew my suspicions before the (inconclusive) embryo's father.

"Oh my God," Dana said.

Dana agreed to go in and buy me another pregnancy test. This time I was explicit in my instructions. "Get the pregnant/not pregnant one," I told her. "The others are inconclusive."

Dana came out with a bag. I shoved it in my purse, then sauntered back into Walgreens, muttering something to the nice woman about having to pee really badly and praying I wouldn't be busted for shoplifting. Or reported to the tabloids for being pregnant. Before I even mentioned the possibility to my husband.

I took the test, and this time it was . . . conclusive. I came out to Dana. "I'm pregnant," I told her. "Pretend you don't know. And never mention that shit transfer to anyone." At this point, now that I have four children, it may seem like I'm always getting pregnant, but at the time Stella was three. I hadn't been pregnant for three years. It was shocking news. *Oh my God.* I texted Mehran: *"it's conclusive. I'm pregnant."*

Now I had this great secret from Dean. We were in the middle of filming our show. Every day there were cameras surrounding us. If there was ever a time to surprise him with a pregnancy, this was it.

There was one more person who had to know my secret: Megan, who worked for World of Wonder, the production company we were partnered with for *Tori & Dean*. Megan was a producer, but we'd also become close friends.

Since Megan was my friend, she congratulated me when I gave her the still-very-confidential news. But she was also my producer, so of course the next text to pop up on my screen was, *"how are we going to play this out on the show?"*

I loved the idea of surprising Dean . . . on camera. When I had taken those first pregnancy tests with Mehran it had been Valentine's Day. Wouldn't it have been cute and romantic for the show if I had surprised Dean that very day?

Fortunately, Dean and I had postponed our exchange of Valentine's presents. We planned to film it for the show, and we'd delayed it for two days because opening the store had been enough for one day (plus I'd gone home sick). Now I had a perfect gift for him.

Keeping the secret from Dean was easier said than done. When I met Dean I went from sharing nothing with my partner to telling Dean everything. TMI is the story of our lives. We regularly share the size, color, and length of our shits. We beckon each other to the toilet to lean in and get a good look. Unfortunately, our kids have picked up on this habit too. There are photos on my phone of the most impressive McDermott family shits. Instagram, eat your heart out.

So keeping my pregnancy from Dean was crazy hard. I wanted the suspense. But I wanted him to ask. I couldn't stand his not knowing. Especially since other people knew. Filming the surprise right meant cluing in a few key people. The five-person crew needed to know what was coming so they could anticipate camera positions, lighting, etc. As a producer I wanted it on camera, but as a wife and mom it felt completely wrong. Over the next two days I found myself dropping hints left and right.

"Babe, I'm really not feeling good. I'm so nauseated." I amped up the moaning and groaning, hoping he would guess my little secret, but to no avail. My ailments were so par for the course he never thought twice about it.

Before we shot the big surprise scene with Dean, we wanted to show me taking the jenky inconclusive pregnancy tests. So Mehran and I did it again, this time in front of the cameras. We stayed as close as possible to what actually happened, except for one thing. In real life, I never shut the bathroom door when Mehran's around. We'll be talking about designs for Little Maven, our children's clothing line, while I take care of business. He doesn't care. What's the big deal? But we couldn't be so . . . *real* for reality TV. (Sort of like the olden days, when they didn't show husband and wife sharing a double bed. Someday, for better or worse, the bathroom doors of sitcom couples and reality stars will be flung wide open for the world to enjoy. Mark my words.) But this time I had to show the test to Mehran by passing it underneath the door. And we also had to accommodate Mehran, who isn't an actor. We had to do several takes before he could muster a big enough reaction, although to this day he'll say, "I did it in two takes, bitch. Nailed it."

The next day we filmed all day. The last scene of the day was to be our reenactment of Valentine's Day, where Dean and I would exchange gifts. The scene started with me in bed. Dean walked in. I asked how the end of opening day had gone at InvenTORI, and I told him I felt bad that I'd had to leave.

Then we got down to business. I went first, opening Dean's present for me, a beautiful diamond heart necklace, set in rose gold.

For Dean's present I'd taken the pregnancy test that said "pregnant" in no uncertain terms, put it in a long, rectangular bracelet box, and gift-wrapped it. When Dean opened it, he was completely surprised. I remember having a half-out-of-body moment. The wife part of me was excited and eager to celebrate with my husband, and the producer in me was outside of my body, watching our exchange, noting his reaction, thinking about how well it would play on TV. This is something I've gotten used to in the course of making reality TV. I can be in the present, but at the same time, in the back of my head, I'm seeing it as a story. The producer side of me reminds me of my dad. He always thought in terms of the narrative. The difference is that he was never in front of the camera at the same time.

Dean was truly surprised and very happy. We hadn't used birth control all those three years, so there was no planning involved. We just felt like our angels came to us when they were ready. Later, Dean confessed that when he saw the shape of the box I had for him, he thought it contained a pen. I was offended. "I give the best gifts. I'm so creative!" I said to him. "I would never in a million years give you a pen!"

Dean just shrugged. "I thought a pen would be pretty cool." He's out of his mind. I like to go big on Valentine's Day. Our third baby? Now, that was my kind of present.

Reality Tweaks

I was pregnant with my third child, and the network wanted to make the pregnancy the focus of the sixth season of *Tori & Dean*.

This wasn't a total shock to me. The season before we'd also shifted the focus late in the game. That season, Dean and I were going through a difficult time. My main complaint was that he was spending full days riding his motorcycle when I thought he should be home with the kids. I felt like he'd kind of checked out of family life. At first we tried to keep our fights, which were getting pretty gnarly, off camera, behind closed doors. Then one day we were sitting around with our director and two producers when Dean and I started fighting. It started with the mo-

torcycle racing. Dean stood up—he was pissed and yelling. I got up too. The crew started to file out of the room
to give us our space. But then, out of the corner of my
eye, I saw Bobby, the director, gesturing with his hand.
He mouthed, "Can we film this?"

I shrugged. Sure. Why not? It was real; couples fight.
Bobby slipped out of the room and came back moments
later with one of our cameramen. To me, it didn't feel like
an invasion of privacy. If anything, it was the opposite. I
was having a hard time standing up for what I wanted. I
felt like I wasn't voicing my needs. Having other people
around felt somehow safer. Also, I always wanted the show
to be real, and it didn't get any realer than this.

In season five, after they had filmed that fight, the
whole rest of the season shifted focus. It became about our
relationship. Dean and I were fighting. The only problem was that we'd already shot a significant chunk of the
season while keeping our issues out of sight. On camera
we were fine and off camera I was telling Megan, our producer, that he was angry all the time and I couldn't deal
with it. That first fight, the one they caught on camera,
was in episode five! It looked like it came out of nowhere.
We needed to show viewers what had been leading up to
it. So we had to go back and see if there was any earlier
footage of us fighting.

In the beginning of the season Dean and I had been

visiting Patsy, the baby nurse who had become a family member, at her home outside Atlanta after she'd had gastric bypass surgery. Looking back at the footage, we found a moment when there was tension between me and Dean and added it in to establish the first signs of trouble.

Just as we had shifted last season to focus on our marital woes, we now wanted the sixth season to focus on my third pregnancy. World of Wonder, Dean, and I wanted to do it in real time—in the third episode of the season—but the network thought that the season premiere should be the amazingly dramatic Valentine's Day during which Dean and I opened InvenTORI, I found out I was pregnant, and I surprised my husband with the news. That meant condensing and cutting much of what we'd already shot for season six. The biggest loss for me was our coverage of my goddaughter Simone's birth.

The fifth season of *Tori & Dean* had ended with me and Dean renewing our wedding vows on our fourth wedding anniversary. After the ceremony, my friend Scout told us that he and Bill had found a birth mother.

The truth was that we'd known about the birth mother for months. She was already eight months pregnant! But Scout and Bill were superstitious, so they wanted to wait to talk about the pregnancy on the show. I understood. We knew that by the time the final episode aired, my goddaughter Simone would have already been born.

Simone was born outside New York between the fifth and sixth seasons of *Tori & Dean* (I'm pretty sure that's not how her Wikipedia entry will describe it). Although the sixth season wasn't under way, I thought our first moments with Simone were important and campaigned for Oxygen to film Scout and Bill's first days as fathers, as they learned to change her, dress her, and feed her. We filmed their moms visiting Simone for the first time—all the things new parents go through.

The day after they got back to L.A., we filmed Liam and Stella meeting Simone, and Bill and Scout asking us to be her godparents. (I was hoping for the honor but not counting on it. But—come on—I was a shoo-in!) We filmed Simone's baptism. We filmed me and James planning her Sip and See party. Instead of having a baby shower, people came to meet the baby and drink cocktails.

We'd already filmed two episodes. The whole first episode was supposed to be catching up on our lives. It showed Simone's birth, us finding the storefront for InvenTORI, renovating the space, and starting to set up that business. The second episode centered on Simone's Sip and See. When we shifted the focus of season six, we lost almost all of Simone's story line. Our viewers had watched Bill and Scout get married on the show. The Guncles had talked about wanting a baby for years. Viewers had seen them trying to adopt and finding a birth mother. Now it was finally happening. Their dream had come true. I wanted the show to follow through. It felt wrong and sad to leave my goddaughter on the cutting room floor, but such is the reality of reality TV.

WE HAD ONE more party left to film for *celebraTORI*, and it was my favorite: Caftan and Cocktails. I couldn't wait to have a party that was a throwback to old Hollywood midcentury modern mixed with loungey Palm Springs resort style from the sixties. A chic party where I got to wear a fabulous caftan. What could be better? In fact, it's possible that the whole reason I did a party-planning book was so that I'd have a good excuse to throw that party. But I had terrible morning sickness. They put me on an IV drip for fluids and a Zofran pump—a mini-catheter that gave me a steady infusion of antinausea medication.

When the day of the Caftan and Cocktails party came, I unplugged myself from my medical assembly and tried on caftans. I had several gorgeous ones to choose from, but I hadn't considered the IV site on my arm. The needle was taped there, ready for me to rescrew the bag of fluid in. I needed a caftan that would cover that arm, and there was only one that would do the trick. It was a gorgeous Roberto Cavalli number that was one-shouldered. That caftan had been a present from our World of Wonder producers, who gave it to me to wear to my vow renewal (possibly a bribery gift to convince me to remarry my husband on my fourth anniversary instead of my fifth in spite of our unresolved issues). I loved the caftan, but I'd already worn it to the vow renewal. I was a little ashamed to give it a repeat performance. Such a Hollywood fashion faux pas. But there was nothing to be done. I also didn't get to buy caftans for my friends; instead we had to raid my closet. So I wasn't the only one who had to wear a repeat caftan. Sacrilege.

With all the parties I've ever thrown—for my children, on the show, for the party-planning book—I've loved the planning. I have a vision of how I want everything to look. But again I was too sick to help much, and I hadn't told anyone that I was pregnant. So this time I arrived an hour before the party, moved a few things around, and felt sad that this—my favorite party—had gotten the least of my attention. James picked up the props all by himself and then set them in place—I couldn't bear to miss that! A food stylist made everything without my watching (although later I did find a moment to redistribute the chopped chives on the deviled eggs). I always breathed down everyone's neck. In a friendly way.

We planned to tell our friends about the pregnancy on camera at the party. Mehran was the only one who already knew. Just before we shot the scene I realized that Ryan, one of the cameramen, hadn't been there the day I told Dean. He didn't know what he was about to shoot. People appearing on camera during a reality show are often surprised by what goes down, but usually the crew has some idea of what's going on. Ryan was in position, camera raised, when I pulled him aside.

"By the way," I whispered, "what you're about to film—I'm pregnant!"

He mouthed, "Congrats," then he raised his camera back up and I dashed back to the poolside bar for the announcement and champagne toast.

Scout was a little annoyed that he had to find out on the show. Afterward, off camera, he said, "I'm really happy for you and this is great news. But, bitch, I'll be mad if I have to find out about your fourth pregnancy on camera!"

OUTSIDE THE SMALL circle of our friends and reality crew, the rest of the world didn't know about my pregnancy. But, as we all know, pregnancies can't be kept secret forever. At least not in Hollywood.

When I was almost three months pregnant, Dean and I hosted a book signing at InvenTORI for the Fabulous Beekman Boys, the city boys turned farmers turned reality stars and lifestyle brand whose soaps and other products we were going to carry at InvenTORI. It was so fun for me to do an event where it wasn't *all about me.*

There had been some speculation in the tabloids about my being pregnant. It was true that I had a little belly, but I planned to wear two pairs of Spanx and a cute frock. The paparazzi would see me and be amazed at how trim I was, and I'd buy myself another month in hiding.

Then, in the days leading up to the party, I popped. By the night of the event, none of the dresses I'd planned to wear still fit. No problem. I found a black shift dress with ruffles. I'd wear it with high-ass heels. My legs would steal all the attention away from my camouflaged belly.

Two hours before the party I got an e-mail from the Beekman boys. They are famous for wearing wellies. They wear their tall rubber boots everywhere—on their farm, with suits, to black-tie events. They would be wearing them to our party and they wanted us to wear them too. There went the high-heel scheme. Now I'd be wearing a shift dress with tall flat rain boots. *Well,* I thought, *at least the dress is black and the boots are Missoni.*

The next day, all over the press, there were pictures of me bending over in my dress with a circle around my belly and the headline "Tori Spelling, obviously pregnant." And I thought I had everyone fooled.

It was time for me to come clean. I'd been down this pregnancy-reveal road a couple times already, and while

I knew my news wasn't going to change anyone's life, I still wanted to keep it private for as long as I could. It was such an intimate, personal truth. I lived such a public life. Before I announced it on Twitter, I had a moment. *This is it. My last moment holding on to something that's mine and mine alone.* I posted my tweet and the news was out.

Soon after we came out, Mehran and I were on a flight home from some business trip. I hadn't had a sip of wine in my first trimester, but I was so nervous about flying that I wanted a little glass of wine to help calm my nerves. But I was pregnant, and there are conflicting opinions about whether any alcohol whatsoever is okay during pregnancy. Even though I had my doctor's sign-off on a glass of wine every now and then, I didn't want to be judged. When the flight attendant offered us drinks, Mehran ordered a glass of sauvignon blanc. I gave him a piercing look.

"And a glass of the . . . pinot noir?" He glanced at me. I smiled approvingly. He knows I'm a red-wine girl. "I want to taste both, I have a craving for red as well," he said.

"I'll have a ginger ale, please," I said, smiling virginally.

The flight attendant brought our drinks. As soon as she walked away, Mehran handed me the red and we quietly clinked glasses. Victory. (Disclaimer: lest I sound too boozy, the in-flight glasses are the size of shot glasses with stems.)

When we were done, the flight attendant returned, the

two bottles cradled in her arms. She offered Mehran a refill, and he accepted. Then she said, "And would we like another glass of that delicious pinot noir, Ms. Spelling?" She winked conspiratorially. Busted.

NOT EVERYONE WAS so accepting of my apparently controversial stance on occasional wine while pregnant. But in my second trimester I craved red wine and would once in a while drink half a glass at dinner. I remembered the press giving Gwyneth Paltrow a hard time for drinking a Guinness while pregnant, so I always had Dean or Mehran order the wine and I'd sip from theirs.

That summer we went to Vegas for an appearance. Dean, Bill, Scout, and I had dinner at a super-fancy steak house owned by Mario Batali. The waiter came over. After he welcomed us, he swept my wineglass off the table with a flourish and walked away with it.

It pissed me off. Who was he to decide that I didn't want wine?

Scout said, "I hate wine. You can have my glass." He slid his glass over so it was in front of me.

The waiter came back to hand us menus. When he was done, he looked down at me, grabbed Scout's wineglass from in front of my place, and walked away with it! The first time was understandable. He saw that I was pregnant and figured I didn't want a drink. Now it was personal. But of course I couldn't confront him. For the rest of the night I took furtive sips out of my friends' glasses, seething. It was a cruel world where my secrets were not mine alone anymore, and a pregnant gal couldn't even get a drink.

On the Bright Side,
Julia Roberts Knows I Exist

Life went on: my morning sickness gradually faded; we continued filming for our show; Stella and Liam trotted off to preschool every morning. Dean and I had struck a nominal peace with the paparazzi who continually lurked outside our house. (Any time we moved, no matter what name we did it under, a self-proclaimed stalker website immediately published our new address and photos of the house, and offered copies of the key for sale. Okay, I'm exaggerating about the key, but it wouldn't have shocked me.) We knew most of the lurkers by face, and usually they were pretty respectful. Once or twice when they had started to follow us, Dean leaned out the window and said, "Please. We're taking our kids to school, and we don't want people to know where it is," and they left us alone.

There was one morning when a cameraman I didn't recognize started to follow me. I tried to lose him while being safe, but the kids were in the car so there was no way I could pull any fancy moves. I finally thought, *This is bullshit.* I turned down a side street and pulled over. The photographer parked behind me. I got out of the car, locked the doors, and walked toward his car. He immediately hopped out and started taking pictures.

I said, "Look, I'm driving my kids to school. Please respect that. If you want to take a picture of me, that's your prerogative, but please don't let it affect my children. Just let me take them to school. I'll be right home after I drop them off. Follow me then—I don't care."

He said, "Okay. Thanks for being so reasonable about it." Then he got in his car and drove away. See? Everyone shares a universal desire to protect the children. It gave me a slightly warm feeling.

But a few months later, in June of 2011, I changed my tune. I was about five months pregnant with Hattie, so I had a belly. Dean was off at culinary school for the day—he was taking a final cooking test to pass a course—and I was driving Liam and Stella to their preschool. I saw someone follow us from the house. At first I thought, *I'm sure he knows where we're going. He'll stop at some point.* But he stayed with us all the way to school.

Was this paparazzo about to take pictures of my children and their sweet, homey preschool? This was unprecedented. The kids' school felt like sacred ground. We lead a pretty public life, but so far the press had never reported the name of the kids' school or shown pictures of them there.

Legally, the paparazzi can't trespass, so once we were on school property, we'd theoretically be safe. The drop-off at the preschool was an open, circular driveway with a parking lot on one side of it. It's also against the law for the paparazzi to take pictures of private property, even if they're standing on public property, but they violate that all the time. The driveway was sort of outside the main gate of the school, and I was worried that he'd decide it didn't count as private.

Indeed, as I nosed into a parking spot, the photographer jumped out of his car and started running toward us, taking pictures as he came. There was a huge sign over the entryway saying the name of the school. If he took pictures of the kids as they passed under that sign, everyone would know where they went to school! *Fuck.* I had to get out of there, and fast.

I threw the car into reverse. I was going to back out quickly, zoom out of the lot, lead him away, and try to persuade him to leave us this modicum of privacy. However, things didn't go as planned. In my panic, I hit the gas too hard. The car leapt backward—straight into a stone wall.

We hit that wall very hard. I was thrown back, then forward. My heart was pounding. Oh my God. Liam and Stella, in the backseat, immediately started chirping, "Mom! You hit the wall!"

I turned around. "Are you guys okay?" They looked comfortable and cheerful in their car seats. They were fine, but they were very excited about the drama of the moment and continued to discuss the amazing news that we'd hit the school.

As I sat in the front seat, still stunned, people started running out of the school. The head of the school. The office staff. But then the most amazing thing happened. A group of moms were standing outside the school. They had witnessed the accident, and all at once, as a group, they started running toward my car. They descended on the paparazzo, who was starting to take pictures of the rear end of my car, smashed up against the wall. (Talk about adding insult to injury.) The moms pushed between him and my car, waving their arms in the air to block his shots. I heard them yelling, "Get out of here! We're going to get you!" Tears of gratitude sprang to my eyes. They weren't even moms I was friends with, but they had formed a mom lynch mob in my defense. My heroes! The photographer yelled at them, determined to get his shot regardless of what had just happened, but finally he gave up and left. Moms in sweats unite! Go mom warriors!

I'd had a few fender benders, but this was by far the biggest accident I'd ever been in. I had hit the wall of the driveway so hard that I'd taken part of it down. The back of my car was crushed, and it was completely undrivable. We ushered the kids inside and saw them to their classrooms. Only after they were out of sight, and I was in the safety of the headmaster's office, did I burst into tears.

The headmaster said, "Are you hurt?"

I said, "No, I'm just so sorry I did this to you. You have this sweet family school. You shouldn't have to deal with this."

The school was meant to be a haven. They didn't deserve this intrusion. And a busted wall. The headmaster was gracious—he and everyone else blamed the paparazzo—but I was mortified.

A friend came to pick me up. We were going straight to the doctor to make sure the baby was okay. As I waited for my ride, my mortification turned to anger. I'd had some faith in humanity, but that guy ruined it. Everyone was just out for a cheap buck. I went on Twitter and wrote: "Paparazzi chased me w/the kids 2school. I was trying to get away from him and had a pretty big accident. Took down whole wall of school. He thn STILL got out to try to get pics. 10 school moms chased him away. Wht will it take? Someone dying for paparazzi to stop? Going to dr now to check on baby. I think its just shock." That tweet was a big mistake. I didn't do it to get attention—I did it to vent and prevent—but a media shitstorm ensued.

It was on every station. Paparazzi and the stars. Children and privacy. Where was the line? I agreed that it was an important issue. But as I watched the coverage I was increasingly horrified. Camera crews stood in front of the preschool. It was night, and the lights were on the reporter as she told the story. "Tori Spelling was in a car accident"—the camera zoomed in on the wall that I'd hit—"while at her children's school." The camera swooped up to the name of the school. There it was. The very shot I'd been so desperate to avoid. They were reporting on how the paparazzi violated privacy without realizing that what they were doing was actually worse. Some tabloid shot of the school would have come and gone, but now it was all over the national news.

On *20/20*, at some red-carpet event, they were interviewing Julia Roberts. It was such topical news that they asked her opinion on the matter. She said something like, "Yes, I think it's terrible." Julia Roberts knew about my car accident! She knew who I was. *Mystic Pizza* was my fave. Every cloud has a silver lining.

I'm the Stalker
You Let in Your Front Door

Julia Roberts was impressive, but she was not on my Must Meet One Day list. Kelly Wearstler, designer extraordinaire, was, and I was about to have my big chance with her.

Two years earlier, Dean and I had spent an ill-fated summer in Malibu, when jury duty, travel, and my own neuroses got in the way of a relaxing vacation. After that experience, I had vowed I would never go to Malibu again. But as summer approached, my two internal voices went to war with each other. The Lucy voice, with its harebrained ideas, said, "Go to Malibu! The sunshine! The waves! The family all crowded together in a tiny beach house!" Then the Ricky voice chimed in:

"You shouldn't be doing this. Remember what happened last time?" Back and forth, back and forth, like a therapy session in my head. I should know better by now. Lucy always wins.

We rented a little house in Malibu: Dean, the kids, and me with my round belly. It was all we could afford, but I was glad the house was small. At home in Encino, our six-thousand-square-foot house was far too big. We were always in different rooms. Here we were all together, on top of each other, and I was in heaven. It didn't hurt that this particular small house was snugly nestled on millionaire row—the Pacific Coast Highway is probably the most expensive highway in the world. But in my mind we weren't leading a grand lifestyle. I did tons of cooking. The kids and I made plaster-of-Paris footprints and other beachy crafts. We were enjoying a cozy family life—cooking, crafting, and watching movies together. It was the life I wanted.

Actually, the life I wanted was right next door. Our immediate neighbor happened to be the fabulous Kelly Wearstler. I'll confess that when we were looking for a summer place, we were shown two houses. The house that I picked worked well for our family, but I definitely factored in Kelly Wearstler's proximity. I mean, Kelly Wearstler is one of my favorite interior designers. I'd loved her from afar for a long time. Spending a summer next door to her—I could see us chatting on the beach while our kids built luxury sand castles together.

I'd say, "Kelly, I love what you've done with malachite."

She'd reply, "Thanks, Tori. What do you think the next stone in design is going to be?"

"You must do tiger's-eye, Kelly."

"Tori, you are a genius."

Then we'd air-kiss and frolic in the sand in matching BFF caftans. (Too seventh grade?) "So lucky," we would say. "If we hadn't been neighbors we might never have met!" Failing that, I would be excited just to say hi on the beach once or twice and bask in her fabulousness for a summer. We even had an in—my friend Cheyenne.

Cheyenne was our occasional masseuse (We're mommy friends, I swear. We double date with our husbands. Does that make it sound less fancy? I'm not talking weekly massage! Just biweekly. Kidding), and she also worked on Kelly. I was always not-so-subtly probing to find out what she was like. Now that she was next door—well, I upped my game. Trying to be discreet, I offhandedly mentioned to Cheyenne that Kelly was next door, and that we both had kids, so if she ever wanted to have a playdate . . . Cheyenne could give her my e-mail. That's right. I was that person.

All July I kept an eye out for signs of life at the Wearst-ler house, but for the first couple weeks we were in Malibu, it seemed to sit cold and empty. Then one day I heard laughter coming from the beach nearby. The Wearstlers had arrived. Their kids were running around on the sand. This was my golden opportunity, but I couldn't rise to the occasion. I was too shy to look in their direction, much less to go over and say hi. Instead, I slunk inside and glanced back as the screen door closed behind me. I caught a glimpse of someone with a wide-brimmed hat and flash of long, golden hair. It had to be Kelly.

Days passed. If I was ever going to meet her, I needed a plan. I brought Mehran in on it.

"Why don't you take a walk on the beach?" he suggested. "Or go to her door and introduce yourself. Borrow something—an egg. Or maybe a slab of agate."

Mehran was full of potential meet scenarios, but I couldn't execute. I was much more comfortable stalking from afar. The closest I came was one day when we were out on the beach and I noticed Kelly's sons playing Frisbee nearby.

"See the two boys playing Frisbee?" I said to Liam and Stella. "You should join in!" But no. They just wanted to keep playing in the sand. Foiled again.

Then one day it finally happened. I walked out onto the balcony and heard a pleasant voice calling out from the balcony next door. I couldn't respond. I scurried back inside. Dean was standing there, looking at me.

"Isn't that Kelly Wearstler calling you? Why aren't you answering her?" he said.

"Um, I think she's talking to someone else," I said. "She's saying 'Cory.'"

Dean peeked out the window. "She's standing right there," he said.

I looked out the sliding door. There she was, waving and saying hi. I stepped back out onto the balcony. So nervous.

Kelly was standing on her nearby balcony. She had long blond hair. She was wearing a cuffed blouse, really short turquoise jean shorts, silver high-tops, and bangles. She held a parasol and didn't seem to have any makeup on. I could tell that this outfit was something that she just threw on for a casual day at the beach. It wasn't something she had carefully put together. I loved her throw-on look. I loved everything about her.

Kelly said, "You have kids my kids' age, right?" Cheyenne had delivered!

"Yes, I think that's right," I said, so coy.

Kelly said, "Bring them over if you want."

I said, "Now?"

She said, "Sure, just come in on the street side. I'll meet you there."

Here it was. The invitation I'd been waiting for. Not only would I meet Kelly Wearstler, I would get to see her

beach house. With her in it. It was the chance of a lifetime. But I couldn't do it.

"Dean, can you walk them over?" I said. But no, Dean
claimed to be in the middle of making lunch. As if lunch
mattered at a time like this.

Oh my gosh. Was I dressed okay? I was wearing maternity jean shorts, a short-sleeved white peasant top from
Forever 21 in size 10, and short fringed Uggs. If I was
going to go through with this, I thought I should change
into something a little more worthy. But what if she'd seen
what I was wearing and figured out that I'd changed my
clothes? That would be the worst. Still, maybe she hadn't
noticed my feet. I threw on a pair of Missoni ballet flats as
a last-ditch effort. I was unfashionable and hugely pregnant. But I was doing this.

HERE'S THE PART that makes me look really creepy. I
had actually been in Kelly Wearstler's beach house once
before. Kelly had let Cheyenne use the house for a day,
and I went over there to see Cheyenne's new baby. Once
inside, I did what I've seen people do when they come
into my house. They pretend to be focused on whatever
business they have with me, but I can see them peering
around corners, trying to get a discreet glimpse of how I
live. The whole time I was at Kelly's house, I was oohing

and aahing over the baby while at the same time internally debating whether to whip out my iPhone to send pictures to Mehran. I didn't want Cheyenne to think I was rude. But Mehran would die when he found out where I'd been. I really wanted to share the moment with him. Prudence prevailed, and I didn't take the pictures.

Anyway, when I finally received the longed-for invitation and came over with the kids, I had already been in Kelly Wearstler's house that one time, and she had no idea. I was the stalker you let through your front door.

I already knew that her house was gorgeous but kind of cold. The walls were covered in beige stone. There were pale hardwood floors that blended with the stone. The palette was relentlessly neutral, with a perfectly calibrated range of textures and colorless patterns. The place was stark and flawless. It was almost impossible to believe that the person who lived there had two boys under ten years old. My kids (and pets) would have spread their toys and crumbs and fur (pets only!) all over that place in five seconds flat.

My kids aren't as socially crippled as I am. As soon as we came in, they peeled off with her kids, and I was left standing with Kelly. A bunch of other guests milled about. It emerged that they were all about to go surfing at Point Dume. Point Dume was known for its surfing and its exclusivity. You could only enter the beach if you lived within a certain triangle and had a key. Kelly had a friend with a key. Of course she did. And Kelly Wearstler was not just an ultrafashionable, megasuccessful businesswoman. She also, unlike me, could head to a private beach, whip out a surfboard, and chill. And here she went. Clearly my vision of us nibbling crudités and chatting about our kids and our mutual passion for design wasn't about to happen. And now that I knew she and her friends were practically out the door, how long were the kids and I supposed to stay? I had no idea what the etiquette of the situation was. All I knew was that I'd probably get it wrong.

As my head spun with all of this, Kelly was perfectly nice and welcoming. Her friends welcomed me too. I didn't know exactly how to start a real conversation, but then I remembered we'd gone to Anguilla and stayed at the Viceroy. I knew that Kelly had designed the Viceroy, along with the interiors of many of the other boutique hotels that her husband's real estate group owned. That had to be a good topic.

"We went to Anguilla and stayed at the Viceroy. It was great." I told her which villa we'd stayed in—I thought it was villa ten.

Kelly said that number ten was a popular one—I remembered that someone at the resort had told us that Michael Jordan had stayed there with his family, and

Chelsea Handler had too (not at the same time as Michael Jordan, though that image was worth something).

I wasn't brave enough to make a joke about Michael Jordan and Chelsea Handler. Nor did I launch into the tale of my encounter with a stray cat at the hotel. Stray cats roam Anguilla, and everyone stays away from them because who knows what diseases they might carry. Naturally, I was the asshole who befriended the stray cat. There was one who lingered outside our villa, meowing woefully at me every day. I put out bowls of water and milk for it. After a couple of days it trusted me enough to come inside for a moment, and eventually it let me pet it. But one night when I went to pet its back, I startled it, and it bit me. It was a stray cat. I was in a foreign country. And I was pregnant, with no idea when I'd last had a tetanus shot. I had to go on antibiotics. None of this ever would have happened to Kelly Wearstler.

She said, "That villa's so great, isn't it?" I agreed, and then there was silence. I was at a loss. The moment was slipping away.

Then Stella announced, "I'm hungry!" Nobody was eating.

"Let's go home and get you something to eat," I said.

"No, no, I'll get her something," Kelly said. She went into the kitchen and brought out some crackers. Uh-oh. Crackers and a three-year-old was a guaranteed crumbfest.

Stella grabbed a big handful. She was going to get crumbs everywhere. That's how Kelly would remember me—as the woman whose child messed up her house. As Stella trotted around, nibbling crackers, I followed her, hunched over, my hands stretched under her chin to catch crumbs, apologizing profusely as I went. Liam was climbing on the couch—shoes off, but still. I told him to get down.

Kelly said, "No, they're kids, it's fine." But was it fine? I couldn't tell.

Then Kelly excused herself to get ready for surfing. As she walked away, I looked down at my Missoni flats, which I had never worn before. They were killing the back of my heel. I had gotten them on sale at Gilt and would never wear them again. Had their one and only wearing been worth it? Had Kelly at least noticed that I was wearing Missoni?

I told Liam and Stella it was time for us to get going. That's where the visit should have ended, with our polite thank-yous and good-byes. We would retreat back to our house with no lasting friendship between me and Kelly Wearstler, but with no damage done beyond a few cracker crumbs on an otherwise speck-free floor. However. My children were having such a nice time that they both immediately fell apart. Liam crossed his arms defiantly and said, "No, I'm not going." He stomped across her beautiful floors.

Liam started wailing, and Stella joined in. I quietly went over and gently took Liam by the arm. "We're guests in this house. I know you're upset, but let's talk about this at home."

He pulled his arm away, and as he did I held on. He screamed, "You're hurting me!" My parenting skills were failing me, and now my child was publicly accusing me of abuse in front of my idol.

What made it worse was that everyone else in the room politely kept talking, pretending that nothing was happening. I knew that was the proper thing to do, but all I wanted was for someone to say, "I feel for you. My kids do this all the time."

My failing attempts to assuage Liam went on for five minutes, which felt like five hours. Kelly tried to help, offering to bring us all with them to surf and showing them videos of her kids in a mini rock band at school. Ultimately, in spite of my efforts to extract my children, we probably overstayed by about half an hour.

We finally left. I still thought she was really cool. And nice. But I had to face reality. There was no magic. She had no real interest in me. Our summer of bonding and subsequent lifelong friendship had begun and ended in one short, awkward hour. Kelly, if you still want my advice on stone trends, I'm standing by.

The Pig Made Me Do It

Even after my fantasy friendship with Kelly Wearstler flopped, I loved our downsized Malibu life. I couldn't help wanting it to go on forever. *How great would it be if we sold our house in Encino and moved to a small house in Malibu?* I thought. The family would be in closer quarters. We'd all spend more time together. We could go to the beach. Then I saw an article in a beach magazine about a chic family with tons of money and an extravagant lifestyle who had moved to Broad Beach, a small (and exclusive) private beach even farther up the coast than we were. This extremely attractive family had downsized from a seven-thousand-square-foot house to a much smaller beach bungalow. The husband and wife talked about how moving to a smaller space brought the family closer. It was terrifying for them at first. They worried about how they'd survive with so much less space. But moving to a beach house had changed their whole lifestyle. Now the tan and beachy mother, who was pictured in gorgeous caftans (my dream!), spent her days surfing with her kids. There was a photo of her cooking while the kids did their home-work at a desk opposite the kitchen counter. The article inspired me. That could be us!

Anyone who knows me knows that as soon as I get a notion like that, well, I have to start looking at real estate listings. We had a whole month in Malibu. It couldn't hurt to peek at a few houses. It started with my poking around online, but before I knew what I was doing, Dean and I were driving up the coast to check out some of the properties. We couldn't afford anything on the beachfront, especially because we needed enough land for the animals.

The animals. Back in Encino, I had what I thought of as a backyard farm.

We'd always had a pack of dogs scrambling underfoot. Then DailyCandy ran a piece on a cool mobile chicken coop for city dwellers. It didn't even kill the grass! I re-minded Dean how planting an organic garden had gotten Liam eating more vegetables. Maybe if we had chickens, and Liam collected eggs, he'd start liking eggs the way he had when he was younger. Dean is always a sucker for a good sales pitch from me. He thought chickens were a great idea.

Then I stumbled across silkie bearded chickens. They have lots of extra-soft fur like poodles and a reputation for being great, sweet pets. And here's another perk of doing a reality show. If you tell them something interests you, the show's staff does all the research. Chris, one of our producers, found adorable silkies at a farm in Norco, California. On Liam's third birthday, we packed up the kids and the crew and went to get chickens. We came home with three. I named one Coco (after Coco Chanel, of course). Liam chose the ultrasophisticated sobriquet Turkey Breast for the second. And Dean, taking a cue in sophistication from his son, named the third Chicken Nugget (but that one turned out to be a rooster, so we returned him).

While on our chicken splurge, we also signed up for a pygmy goat. She would be ours as soon as she was weaned. I initially named her Donna Martin, but by the time she arrived, the joke had worn off and Dean named her Totes McGoats after the movie *I Love You, Man.*

One day we went to the pet store Kahoots to get food for the animals, and they had a bunch of newly hatched chicks. They were irresistible. We brought home five. These we couldn't sex, but only one of them turned out to be a rooster. We kept him and named him Jackson.

For Stella's second birthday that June we got two rabbits. They immediately had twelve babies, ten of whom we gave away. (I identified with the mother rabbit, but I would never give my own away.) And at some point around that time I went to Petco for supplies and brought home a bearded dragon named Princess and a snake. (The snake didn't last long. It became anorexic and wouldn't eat. Apparently this sometimes happens with snakes. The poor thing died of starvation. I was surprised that *Star* didn't pick up on the story for a "pets look like their own-ers" piece.) Then there was another goat. And, around Father's Day, two rescue guinea pigs.

Coco the chicken lived in the house with the dogs. She was trained. Ish. The rest of the chickens were in a chicken coop (not the chic mobile one that had launched the madness). Totes McGoats was smart. She learned to use the doggie door in one day. But it can be hard to house-train goats because they don't really know when they're pooping. But since they only eat oats and hay, goat poop is sweet smelling, and to dogs it's like candy. So the dogs followed the goat around and cleaned up after her. Life on the farm.

Something was clearly going on with me. All this ani-mal expansion happened toward the end of the fifth sea-son of *Tori & Dean*, right when Dean and I were going through relationship strife. My beef was that Dean spent too much time biking or sitting at the computer looking at racing events and gear. Maybe I should have been grateful. At least his concept of porn was racing helmets and riding gloves. He wasn't doing horrible shit, but he was disconnected and quick to anger. There is no doubt that, although we never said it out loud, the animals created chaos and distraction. Instead of focusing on our relationship, there was an ongoing stream of new creatures to take care of. It would take me a while to realize that part of the reason our farm kept expanding was so I could postpone dealing with the issues in our relationship.

THERE WAS ONE more animal occupying a small but rapidly growing space in our backyard farm: the pig. When I heard that there was something called a micro-mini pig, which only grew to be twenty pounds, I envisioned a whole farm of minis right there in the backyard. Dean was on board. New animals were something we usually agreed on. He was always game—at least in the moment; he only got angry later when he had to clean up after them. (I'm really good at cuddling and playing with and loving the animals, but poop scooping isn't exactly my forte.)

Soon after I first read about micro-mini pigs, a friend sent me a link to a listing on Craigslist. It described a little pig named Hank, almost fully grown and still under twenty pounds. The pictures showed him wearing sunglasses and a dog sweater. He was already comfortable wearing clothes! I had to have him. He was going to fit right in. And at four hundred dollars he was much cheaper than the other listings I'd seen, which had micro-minis costing thousands of dollars.

I called the owner right away. At first she said that they had another buyer. I immediately got competitive. When she told me that Hank slept in bed with his owners, I told her that we had a European king and thousand-thread-count sheets. He would love it at our home. (Of course, it's the cotton staple length that matters, not the thread count, but I couldn't go into it with her.)

The owner seemed swayed by my passion. "Can't you come do a home visit? We'll pay more!" I added. I drive a hard bargain.

She agreed to bring him over.

In the photos on Craigslist, Hank was tiny and adorable. When he and his owner arrived at my house, his size surprised me.

"He looks twice as big as he did online," I said to the owner.

"Yeah," she said. "Those pictures are a little old. He's nine months old, though. He shouldn't grow much more."

She had a very sweet scrapbook showing Hank's first months on Earth. Here was an article from his local newspaper showing him at some event. Here he was wearing

a party hat. Here he was dressed up for the holidays, posing on Santa's lap. Hank's owner seemed very attached
to him—she agreed to sell him to us, but she teared up
when it came time to say good-bye. Yet for all her love of
her pig, she was moving to a place that didn't take pigs. It
seemed a little odd, but I'm not one to question.

That night Dean started to set up a dog bed for the
newest member of our family, but I put my foot down.
The owner had said he was used to sleeping in a bed. I
had promised. "He sleeps in our bed," I said. I picked
up all forty pounds of him and carried him up our spiral
staircase. As we ascended, he let out a huge squeal that
echoed throughout the house. I should have taken it as a
cry of warning, but soon enough Hank settled in between
me and Dean, his head nestled in a down pillow, and went
to sleep.

In the middle of the night a noise woke me out of a
dead sleep. I had no idea what it was, but it sounded like
the room was flooding. I sat up in bed. Hank was no longer tucked between me and Dean. He was gone.

I stood up and crept forward. "Hank? Hank?" In the
dark I couldn't see him but I headed toward the sound of
gushing water. There he was, facing the corner, pissing.
Only then did I remember that the owner had warned me
that pigs like to pee in corners of rooms. I wanted to say,
"Hank! Stop!" He needed to be trained not to do this. But

I was afraid that if I interrupted him, he'd turn and spray pee everywhere. Instead, I stood, watching silently as my not-so-micro-mini pig peed on and on. He must have peed for five minutes. By the time he was done, there was a fully soaked circle, two feet in diameter, in the corner of our plush cream wall-to-wall carpeting. I had insisted on cream, even though Dean worried the kids would destroy it. The prospect of corner-peeing pigs had not entered the bedroom-carpet negotiation.

When Hank was done, it wasn't a job for a few paper towels. It was a job for several long-staple Egyptian cotton bath sheets.

As anyone other than me would have realized from the start, Hank was not a micro-mini, if such a thing exists. He wasn't a mini. He wasn't even a potbelly. He was a full-on slaughterhouse pig who would grow to be well over two hundred pounds. Months later, I texted the seller. I wanted to tell her that Hank was going to appear on our show and that he was going to be on the poster promoting it. I thought she'd want to know that he was semifamous. When I sent her the photo, I added, "And by the way, as you'll see, I don't think he's a micro mini."

All she said was, "Oh, I've heard about these scams." But clearly she knew the truth—why else would she have parted with him while he was still relatively little and cute? I knew she still loved him. Why else would she sign her texts "Hank's mom"? (Why would anyone sign their texts anyway?)

We had two goats, five chickens, one rooster, four dogs, a bearded dragon, a guinea pig, and four rabbits, and we were doing fine. But Hank really needed to be on a farm. Perhaps house-hunting for a farm in Malibu was a bit rash, but all I can say is that I did it for Hank. The pig made me do it.

THE ANIMALS WERE a critical part of this new fantasy that quickly became my obsession. As we worked our way up the coast and started looking up in the canyon, we began to find farms. It was amazing! You could live on the west side, be near the beach, and have a farm with horses and chickens. The prices (I convinced myself) weren't as crazy if you just drove a bit farther north and inland. We could really do this. We could sell our house, move into a smaller house for less money, and live out my months-long dream of being a farmer.

That September we went into escrow on a house. It was a little house. When I said we were downsizing, I wasn't kidding. This house was fifteen hundred square feet, a quarter the size of our house in Encino. It was barely big enough to hold our family, but what did that matter—it was a tear-down anyway. What made it desirable was that it was built on one acre of great property. You stepped out of the kitchen to a glorious view of the whole coastline. The land surrounding the house was full of lavender and fruit bushes. I pictured myself in a chic brimmed hat, holding a wire basket, picking lavender. I would sew little sachets, filled with lavender from my backyard and tied with twine, and give them as Christmas gifts. I saw myself making jam from the kumquats and tangerines. Hank and the chickens would have the run of the horse ring. (There was a horse ring.) And this whole perfect setup was really underpriced because the old woman who lived there needed to sell it.

We didn't talk about the fact that one day whatever money we had saved in the price would have to go toward tearing down the house and building a new one. And we also wanted a pool. The kids would die without a pool. But since we couldn't afford to rebuild the house, much less install a pool, it would have to be a plunge pool out front. I learned that in Malibu it takes eighteen months to get building plans approved, but even that didn't daunt me. My plan was to move our whole family, including the newborn, to the tiny, ramshackle, two-bedroom house while we waited for plans to be approved. Part of me was thinking that it would make a hell of an episode, or even an entire season, of *Extreme Makeover: Home Edition*, McDermott-style.

Lucky for us, it turned out that until we sold our house in Encino, we had no money for the down payment. We had to back out of escrow. That would have been a great moment to let go of this fantasy, return to the Valley, and continue life on our suburban animal farm. But I was unstoppable.

A week later we found my dream house. Or what I convinced myself was my dream house. It was a single-story bungalow in Point Dume, on the beach side of the highway, with a beach access key. Take that, Kelly Wearstler! It was five minutes by golf cart from the private beach—no paparazzi!—and it was on two acres. We could certainly have a farm on two acres! What else could we possibly need?

The house, at 2,200 square feet, was about four thousand square feet smaller than our current house. There were only three bedrooms—one for us, one for Hattie and Patsy (her baby nurse), and one for Liam and Stella. Where would my stepson, Jack, sleep? Dean thought he'd like the trailer that came with the house, parked in the yard. I wasn't so sure. But we did want to downsize.

There were a few other small issues. I didn't like the bamboo floors—but we could replace them with reclaimed wood. There was no air-conditioning—but at the beach nobody had air-conditioning. We'd have the breeze from the ocean. There was no pool—but someday when we had fifty grand to spare, we could build a pool. The house was small—but one day we could add a second level. It was on two acres of land, much of which was wild—but one day we could clear it and have the farm of our dreams.

The house had just fallen out of escrow, and the owner's real estate agent told us we had to act fast. It would be sold again by the end of the day. There was no need to do inspections—they'd all been done by the buyers who were pulling out. And why were the buyers pulling out? Oh, it was just a money thing for them.

I spoke to my best friend, Jenny, who is always a voice of reason. When she heard that the house was in Point Dume, prime Malibu real estate in a great school district, she said, "My dream is to live in Point Dume! It has the best school. I'd move my whole family just to send the kids there, to be near the beach, and to still be near the west side. I'm so jealous." Jenny thought it was a good idea. That sealed the deal.

I asked my mother to lend us the money for the down payment until our house in Encino sold. I told her it was my dream house, a once-in-a-lifetime opportunity. She agreed. We were moving to Malibu.

It's a ~~Boy~~ Girl

Of all the psychic, spiritual, voodoo gurus in my world, Cindy was the most consistently accurate. A year before I got pregnant with Hattie, she had said, "You're going to get pregnant next year with your third child."

I said, "Really!" This came completely out of the blue. It had been two years since Stella was born.

Completely matter-of fact, she said, "You'll get pregnant in January or February, and it's going to be a boy."

I had been shocked to find myself four weeks pregnant with Hattie on Valentine's Day, and then I remembered. *Cindy predicted this.*

Since Dean and I had a boy and a girl at home, we told

Dr. J from the start not to reveal our third baby's gender. Besides, we already knew it was a boy. If Cindy was accurate enough to call the month of conception, then surely she was right about the gender. I was having a boy.

The entire world agreed with Cindy. When I walked down the street, strangers came up to me, patted my belly, commented on my shape or the way I was carrying, and said, "Oh, you're so cute. Boy, right?" Every person, from close friends to car valets, was utterly confident it was a boy. The only person who thought I was having a girl was my mother, but I wasn't about to listen to her.

As we prepared to move to Malibu, I started decorating the room that would be the baby's nursery. I had the walls painted gray; I ordered a gray crib and a gray and white patterned chair. I was going to have yellow bedding and giraffes in the nursery. People told me I was crazy to order anything before the baby was born, but I kept saying that if it was a boy, I'd add pops of turquoise, and if it was a girl, I'd add pops of fuchsia. It would all work out. Because we were having a boy. We were going to call him Finn, a name Dean and I both loved and had planned on if we ever had another boy.

I had a Cesarean scheduled for a week before my due date. Once you've had two C-sections, they make you have a third, and so on. Two weeks before my due date I woke in the middle of the night. I'd had a sharp pain.

Was it a contraction? I sat up to see if anything else would happen, and that's when I felt a tiny bit of pee. Oops. I started to get out of bed to go to the bathroom.

Stella and Liam both happened to be sleeping in our room that night. We'd had some sleep issues lately. The children seemed to want more time with us in anticipation of the new baby coming soon. Often if they wanted to sleep with us we'd put two comforters and two pillows on the rug next to my side of the bed. We called it their fort. If I wanted to get out of bed in the middle of the night, I'd scoot to the end of the bed so I didn't step on them.

Now that I was full-term, I couldn't scoot to the end of the bed anymore. Instead, I carefully placed one tiptoe on the floor between the side of the bed and Stella. Then I put my other foot down. Just then, as I stood above her, it happened. My water broke all over Stella.

Another contraction hit me. Stella slept on, blissfully ignorant of her unfortunate baptism. I went to the bathroom. I could feel contractions, but the last time I'd been in labor was two kids ago, and even then it had been in a hospital setting. I wasn't sure how to handle it.

Maybe I should have woken up Dean. But I'd made the switch from BlackBerry to iPhone and there was a new authority figure in my life. In a panic, I grabbed my phone to ask Siri for help. Was there an application to time my contractions? Siri told me she'd never really thought about it. I decided to find out for myself. I went to the app store, and, sure enough, there were five hundred different contraction timers. Because that is the world we live in.

I downloaded the most expensive contraction-timer app (some of them were free—how reliable could they be?) and started timing my contractions. It was fascinating. I sat in bed, tracking the length of and time between my contractions for about half an hour. At five A.M. I finally woke up Dean. He called Dr. J and told him that my contractions were four and a half minutes apart. He said he'd meet us at the hospital.

I wasn't just a reality-show star. I was a fan, and lately I'd been watching *The Rachel Zoe Project*. Some women had told me that when they were pregnant they liked watching me go through my pregnancy on-screen. I felt the same way about Rachel Zoe's pregnancy.

When Rachel Zoe was in labor, she put on jewelry and fixed her hair. That scene was seared in my brain. If Rachel Zoe bothered to primp in between contractions, I could take the time to make myself presentable.

Think about it, people. What's the likelihood that Rachel Zoe was actually in labor when her husband filmed that scene? Hard to say. I was a reality star, watching a reality star, knowing she might have staged this scenario, but live by the sword, die by the sword. I started putting on makeup, thinking, *I'm gonna do it right this time.*

I wasn't thinking clearly. I hadn't even packed a hospital bag. Dean pulled me away from the mirror and I quickly threw together a few essentials: toiletries, a hospital gown that I designed and had made from fabric I found (which I would never get a chance to wear), pajama bottoms, T-shirt, and socks. I ran and woke up our live-in housekeeper, Susana, to ask her to get in our bed so someone would be there when Liam and Stella woke up. Then Dean threw my bag into the car and we left.

By the time we got to the hospital, I was screaming in pain and begging for an epidural. I'd definitely never had contractions like this.

Dean said, "What about your hospital gown? The gown you made? Do you want it?"

"Fuck the hospital gown," I said.

The nurse said, "Oh my God, you had time to put on makeup?"

I managed to hold it together for a second, smiled, and said, "That's right." Here's to us, Rachel Zoe.

Then they gave me an epidural and we went into surgery.

Dr. J was performing the Cesarean. At some point he said to Dean, "Dad, get the camera ready. The baby's coming." Dean turned on the video camera, and Dr. J lifted up the baby. "All of you were *wro-ong*!" he said in a singsong voice.

"It's a girl!" Dean exclaimed.

Dr. J had known we were wrong about the baby's gender the whole time. How long had he been planning to tease us about it?

"Oh my *God*!" I said. I was utterly shocked. Not one percent of me thought it was going to be a girl. One second later I added, "Oh shit, my mom was right!"

I lay in the recovery room, a little bit out of it. The baby was sleeping on my chest. A nurse came in with a clipboard and asked us the baby's name.

Dean looked at me. I shrugged. We didn't have a girl's name. It was supposed to be a boy, and his name was going to be Finn. "Baby Noname McDermott," he said.

I said to Dean, "Google 'old-fashioned female names' on your phone."

Dean found a list and started reading out names, one by one. When he got to the H's, he read, "Hattie."

At the same time, we both said, "Hattie." That was it. The perfect name for our baby girl.

I told Dean I wanted her middle name to be Margaret, after my nanny who had raised me and had since passed away but was like a second mother to me.

"I love that," Dean said. "Hattie Margaret McDermott."

* * *

WE WEREN'T THE only ones who'd been expecting a boy. Mehran was the first to arrive at the hospital. We didn't tell him her gender. He walked into the room, saw Hattie in my arms, and looked more surprised than I've ever seen him. "Oh my God, it's a girl!" he said. It was such a big, happy reaction from Mehran, who is always so closed off and guarded.

When my mom arrived, the first thing she said was, "I knew it! I told you it was going to be a girl."

I said, "Her name is Hattie."

Later, Patsy would observe that the most famous Hattie was the first Academy Award–winning African-American actress, Hattie McDaniel, who won for playing Mammy in *Gone with the Wind*. Margaret—whom I called Nanny—was also black.

"She's white on the outside, but she's black on the inside," Patsy said. I smiled when she said that. Having grown up with Nanny, watching *The Jeffersons* and *Sanford & Son*, eating the Southern food that she grew up with, and spending summers running around under sprinklers with her community in Crenshaw, I've always said the same thing about myself.

* * *

WE HAD SHIFTED the sixth season of *Tori & Dean* to focus on my pregnancy, so I guess I shouldn't have been shocked when the network told me they wanted the final scene of the season to be me having the baby. I mean, it made sense. But I didn't know if I wanted to film that. It was a little *too* real.

We hadn't filmed Liam's birth—we'd just done a montage of pictures that Dean had taken, played along with some audio from our video camera. We had filmed me going into surgery with Stella, and the rest we did on our personal video camera.

I hadn't decided one way or the other about the birth itself, but we had planned for them to film me being wheeled into surgery again, so I wasn't surprised when the crew went ahead and got clearance at Cedars. But the Cesarean wasn't at its regularly scheduled time. It had all gone down quickly and unexpectedly. As I headed to the hospital I knew we could have called the crew and told them it was happening, but I made the conscious decision not to do it.

Instead, I waited until the last possible moment, when I was about to go into surgery, figuring that when they missed the heading-into-surgery shot and missed the birth, they'd just hold off and wait for us to contact them about what we wanted to film and when. But I was my own demise. When our producer got my text, he alerted the team and they all came straight to the hospital. They were waiting for me when I came out of surgery.

The personal and professional lines had blurred. If I'd contacted a friend, saying I was heading into surgery, she wouldn't have rushed to the hospital without checking with me. But with our crew there was no question or discussion. They already had clearance at the hospital. I never had a chance to change my mind. A mere half an hour after Hattie was born the camera guy, the sound guy, and two producers, Richard and Megan, appeared in my hospital room. They started filming as if it were any other day on the set of *Tori & Dean*. Meanwhile, Mario, one of our camera guys, is an excellent photographer. He had offered to take still photos, just for us, so I did text him after Hattie was born. He came and took some of the first pictures of Hattie. I wanted Mario there, but I didn't want the crew there so soon.

It wasn't a matter of what they filmed or whether and how they used it. I had approval over the material. It was just that they were there. They were there for those first hours when it should have been just me, Dean, Hattie, and whoever we chose to have with us. The camera crew was there when the kids arrived. They were there when my mom came. They were the first people to see my baby. Before all those people and my best friends.

For the first time in six years of filming a reality show,

I felt invaded. I was missing this special day. But I was so out of it and into my baby, I didn't have the wherewithal to turn to these people and say, "Get out of here." Even if I'd been completely clear, it would have been a hard thing to say. They had become friends, after all. I loved that we all felt like a family. We had all intentionally blurred the lines between work and friendship, and I am still close to all of those people, but in that moment I felt like I was nursing my baby in front of business associates. It all felt wrong.

As the epidural wore off, I started throwing up. I looked at Dean. He said something, and the cameras pulled back, but they were still filming from a greater distance. And they stayed. All day. Nobody checked to see if I was okay with it. Maybe at some point I'd said it was fine; I'm not sure. I'd let them film me fighting with Dean. I had let them film my kids having temper tantrums. I had let them film me in my underwear undergoing a spiritual cleanse with a voodoo high priestess. How were they supposed to know this was any different? But it was. Things change in the moment.

I always have a bad reaction after the surgery: a migraine, vomiting, weakness, and just being out of it. I didn't have it together to take charge of the unwanted situation with the film crew, to say the least, but when I was finally alone with Dean, I asked him to tell them to leave. I'd had enough.

It was remarkable that nothing had ever felt intrusive before. Maybe they were crossing more boundaries, or maybe I was changing. But I think of that day, Hattie's birthday, as the beginning of the end of that chapter of *Tori & Dean*.

I DIDN'T HAVE any clothes for Hattie to wear when we brought her home from the hospital. The day before my water broke, Mehran and I had had a "girls'" before-baby day. We had sushi (nothing raw), then went to see the Anna Faris rom-com *What's Your Number?* Afterward, we went to the Juvenile Shop to find something for the baby to wear home from the hospital. We picked out a pile of outfits for girls and boys. Then I looked at this huge pile of clothes and said, "What am I going to do? Buy all this stuff and then return it?" I kept some neutrals, but I put all the pink clothes back. Poor Hattie.

While I was in the hospital, my mother returned everything we had bought, picked up a load of pink clothes, and brought it all back to the hospital.

* * *

FROM MY HOSPITAL bed, with James's help, I reconsidered the gray room that was on order for Hattie's Malibu room. Pops of fuchsia? Forget it. My Hattie needed a pink room. Pink, pink, pink. Pink walls, pink bedding, a pink chair. With a gray changing table, gray carpet, and gray crib. As for the yellow bedding and giraffes? I'd find a use for that sooner than I could possibly imagine.

Fish Out of Water

Hattie was born October 10, 2011, and we immediately packed up to move to Malibu. Randy, my executive producer from World of Wonder, came over to meet Hattie. After the visit, since I was still recovering from the Cesarean, I said good-bye from the top of the stairs instead of walking him to the door. I stood holding week-old Hattie at the top of the overly grand, curved staircase in the entryway of the Encino house. Dean and I hated that staircase. Our producer was at the bottom of the stairs, leaving our house for the last time. He gave one final look around, then turned to look up at me.

"You're going to miss this house," he said. "It was a real family home. To a lot of people." Then he walked out the door. That statement still haunts me. I didn't love that house, but I had no idea what lay in store.

The first ill omen was the jumping cactus. Right before we moved, in the days just after Hattie was born, Dean had decided to prepare our new house for the arrival of our brood by building a chicken coop. It was a kick-ass chicken coop, complete with a run for the chickens and a pen for the goats and the pig. It took him ten days to make it. I was at home nursing Hattie when Dean came back from Malibu, with tiny needles sticking out all over his hands, arms, back, and legs.

"What did you get into?" I asked.

"I have no idea," he said. "I didn't go remotely near any cactus."

Dean gritted his teeth as I used tweezers to pick out the nearly invisible little needles one by one, and we forgot about the incident until we moved to Malibu. A gardener came to check out the yard and tell us how impossibly expensive it would be for us to clear it to make more room for the animals. He'd barely stepped into the yard when he said, "You have a jumping cactus!" Apparently, Dean hadn't bungled into a cactus without noticing after all. Our soft, fuzzy looking cactus was known for "jumping" onto passersby. It had attacked Dean! What a lovely plant for young children. The real estate agents who sold us the house had rhapsodized over the delicious figs and pomegranates we'd soon be plucking from our trees. But somehow they failed to mention the jumping cactus.

The final episode of the sixth and last season of *Tori & Dean* covered Hattie's birth—and ultimately, though it was more than what we'd done for the other two, I thought they edited it very nicely, although I was still bitter about it. Then the final scene showed me and Dean, the children, and the animals all sitting on and around a bench in the backyard of the Malibu house.

I said, "Now, *this* is our dream house."

Dean said, "Good, 'cause I'm not moving again."

After we shot the scene, the crew took a look around our new digs. They commented on how magical our little bungalow was. In the nicely groomed grassy yard were the fig tree, the pomegranate tree, and a blood orange tree. Beyond the yard was a tangle of weeds and tightly matted brush. Everyone kept saying how different it was from what they had expected. I knew what they meant. Encino was all marble and ornate details. This was dramatically smaller, simpler, and rough around the edges. We'd gone from one extreme to another.

"This is the real me," I told them, and I felt a surge of pride. *That's right,* I thought, *Tori Spelling lives in a California bungalow in the wilderness in Malibu.* I liked the sound of it.

* * *

OF COURSE, THERE was a bit of a learning curve to life in the wilderness.

The house, which was so charming with its tidy built-ins and green lawn, was in other ways as rustic as you could get. There were ants and spiders, which were to be expected. There were windows up high on the house that were hard to reach and covered in dust. Well, we were in the country, after all.

Then, on our second night, the heater broke. This didn't seem like an urgent problem until the third night, when the temperature dipped. As I lay in bed listening to the high-pitched howls of a pack of coyotes, an icy draft came through the window frames. I burrowed my feet under Dean, trying to keep warm. I finally drifted off, dreaming of icicles and ice-fishing, but it seemed like only moments later when the early-morning sun burst into the room. I got up to tie a T-shirt over my eyes and climbed back into bed thinking longingly of the silk drapes we'd left back in Encino. They were remote-controlled blackout drapes. I'd never taken the time to appreciate how dark they kept our bedroom. Boy, I'd been living the life.

Other kinks presented themselves. A few nights after the heater broke, the carbon monoxide detector went off. The hot water heater wasn't venting properly. Tori-style, we moved to the Hotel Bel-Air for three nights while we waited for it to be repaired. Then—I'm not even kidding—the refrigerator, washer, and dryer broke in quick succession, and their respective repair people deemed them irreparable. As a special bonus surprise, the air filters were caked with mold. Note to self: always have house inspected no matter what the seller's Realtor says.

The blackout curtains weren't the only past luxury I finally appreciated. It wasn't until we had to buy a new refrigerator that I realized how lucky I'd been to live in houses that came with fancy appliances. A new Viking refrigerator like the one we'd had in Encino cost nine thousand dollars! We couldn't begin to afford it.

One of the few upgrades we'd made to the house before we moved in was to replace the bamboo floors with reclaimed wood. It was expensive, but I was head over heels in love with the look of wide, unwaxed barn-house floors. It never occurred to me that the damn floors would be splinter factories. They were worse than the jumping cactus. The kids kept getting splinters in their feet. Even after we made the rule that everyone had to wear socks or slippers all the time, they still got them in their fingers.

We did remove the man-eating cactus, but the gardener who took care of it bore more grim news about the state of our backyard. I told him I was hoping to clear some space for the kids and animals to run around. He strode across the lawn to examine its overgrown perimeter. When he came back to me, he was shaking his head.

"Well, this is a lot of work you've got here," he said. The grounds were full of huge, dead trees that were fire hazards, he explained. He told me it would be one hundred grand to clean them out.

"Okay," I said. "Can we do it gradually?"

"I don't know, he said, continuing to shake his head. "This is a big job. This is a really big job. I don't know where to start." Wow, even a person who did this for a living had no interest in tackling our yard. It was probably for the best. We couldn't afford it anyway.

Dean and I weren't the only ones who had to make some adjustments. When we told Liam that he and Stella were going to share a room, he was devastated. The former owners had two kids, a boy and a girl. One of the kids' rooms was green, and one was purple. When my kids first saw the house, they figured they'd each have one of those rooms. They hadn't factored in their soon-to-be-born sister. I gently broke it to them that one room would be a nursery for Hattie and Patsy to share, and that the two of them would share the other bedroom. Liam had an insta-meltdown. "I don't want to share a room with Buggy!" he protested. "I want my own room!"

Oxygen was there, filming this moment of disappointment. Later, one of the network executives said to me, "That was so relatable. That was the most relatable you've ever been."

Sigh. Was that the goal? We bought this tiny house, put ourselves in debt, and said good-bye to civilized life as we knew it just so we could be real?

Liam and Stella's room was very small, but I found a way to satisfy them both. I split the room in two visually, putting in two separate carpets and two different wallpapers. Stella's side of the room was pink and purple and white. Liam's was blue, green, and orange. The result was adorable. But we still hadn't answered the question of where Jack would sleep.

There was the trailer in the backyard. From the beginning Dean was convinced that it was perfect for Jack. He said, "When I was a teenager I would have been beyond psyched to have my own trailer." I had my doubts. Maybe if the trailer had resembled the ones I'd grown up with—the double-wides that actors use as dressing rooms on movie lots. They are clean and new, and inside they look like apartments. But our trailer had old wall-to-wall carpet and brown sliding accordion doors. There were cockroaches and spiders. The rickety pile in our backyard didn't fall into my definition of "trailer." The word I would have chosen was "shack."

Jack gave it a shot, he really did. He spent a couple

nights out there, no doubt listening to the same coyotes that kept me up every night. After that he slept on a cot that we wedged in Liam and Stella's room between their two bunk beds. They had to be very careful not to step on Jack when they got out of bed. Dean thought it was fine. "How do you think other people live?" he said. But I don't think other people are crazy enough to downsize so dramatically with three children, a teenager, a baby nurse, and all those animals.

Part of why we'd moved was for the amazing Point Dume schools, but it was the middle of Liam's last year at his preschool, and I wanted him to graduate with the rest of his class. If he was staying, Stella might as well stay too. So every day we drove them from Point Dume to Encino. It was a forty-five-minute drive each way. En route, both children would fall asleep. When we arrived at school, they were cranky and out of sorts. They never wanted to get out of the car.

Our prospects for the fall didn't look much better. Liam could start at the Point Dume kindergarten. But there was no room in the local preschool. It had been booked two years in advance. We had no plan for Stella, other than to keep her at the preschool in the Valley. We were locked into this commute for more than a year.

We tried to make the most of it. One night Dean said, "All I want to do is sit in the back and appreciate the land." He poured us each a drink, and we sat down on the porch.

Our land backed right against parkland. There was no view, just the dark shadows of dense trees. As the sun set, the packs of coyotes began to howl. It seemed like a tumbleweed might roll by. Dean loved it. I wanted the manicured garden that I pictured with a farmhouse in the Italian countryside. I wanted the meticulous grounds of Versailles. You can take the girl out of the manor . . . I looked at the wild bushes, weeds, and cactuses, and sighed.

Dean said, "What? You don't like it?"

I said, "Do you really think I like this?"

Dean said, "I think it's beautiful, but I can't enjoy it if you're unhappy."

I said, "What are we going to do during the summer with no pool?"

Dean said, "I'm going to get an aboveground pool for them."

I said, "What's that? Like a blow-up pool?"

Dean tried to explain, but I had to Google Image it to understand. Understanding is not the same as accepting.

Dean said, "That's what most people do."

On November 16, the night of Dean's birthday, the family went to dinner, and afterward Stella and Liam were in our bed, opening Dean's presents. I was in bed too, wearing just underwear, no top. Dean and Liam started making funny faces and taking pictures of them with Dean's phone. Dean tweeted one of Liam with a rolling-pin sticker from the gift wrapping stuck on his forehead. He captioned it "Pinhead." What he didn't notice was that in the background of the shot, in plain view, were my tits. Oblivious to the impending storm, we went to sleep. At seven thirty A.M. I awoke to our house phone and both cell phones going crazy. It was our publicist calling. My husband had unknowingly leaked (no pun intended) a pic of my milk-engorged nursing boobies to the public. My tits had gone viral.

Dean deleted the photo from his Twitter account right away, but the damage was done. Some people felt bad for me. Others criticized me for having my top off in front of my children. I pled that I was nursing Hattie. But the truth was Hattie had been fast asleep in her room for a couple of hours. I was just topless. Dean and I don't believe in hiding our bodies. We don't want our children to feel that their bodies are something to hide. Also, well, I'm lazy and sometimes can't be bothered to go all the way to the closet to change into nightclothes.

WHEN THANKSGIVING ROLLED around, we still hadn't settled in. Before we moved we had given away boxes and boxes of stuff. We put most of our furniture, which belonged in a much bigger house, in storage. Even so, we still had boxes up to our ears. We were so overwhelmed by the boxes that we put them outside, in a big pile leading down the hill, with tarps covering them. Boxes of toys, shoes, office supplies, files, pictures, and a collection of faux-fur vests that would disappear, never to be seen again. What would we do with these boxes? And when? We had no plan. Nonetheless, I boldly invited my mother to our house for a country Thanksgiving. I wanted to thank her for helping us with the down payment, of course, but part of me also wanted her to see the real me. Her daughter—raised in a mansion—had chosen a simple, small family life.

I was nervous for my mother to see the house. She'd loaned us the money to buy it, and I wanted her to think we'd made a sensible investment. But we'd only been living there for about a month, and the place was still in complete disarray. Even putting the clutter aside, this house was completely contradictory to how my mother lived. In the moments before she arrived I looked at our Thanksgiving setup through her eyes. The kitchen wasn't more than a corner nook. Dean, Patsy, and I were all climbing on top of each other trying to cook. The kids were clamoring to help. I was photographing every step for my blog. It was chaos.

I watched through the window when my mother's driver pulled up. The front yard was filled with weeds.

There was a little stone pathway, with weeds on either side, leading up to a rickety old wooden fence. (It was the white picket fence of my dreams, but at this moment its gate was off its hinges.) My mother approached, holding a bunch of roses and a housewarming gift. She opened the gate, and Hank, the pig, nearly ran her down. The reality show producer in me took mental note. Perfect.

"Hi, Mommy!" I said, stepping out onto the front porch. "Welcome to our new house." What would she say? Would she notice how charming the house was? Or what a big change this was for us?

"Oh my God, is that a pig?" she said. If she had any thoughts about the house and our move, I would have to wait to hear them.

"Yes, you know Hank." I led her to the door, shooing the chickens out of our way. Dean was right there to greet her, as were the kids. There was nowhere else to be. There were still boxes blocking the hallway.

We had Thanksgiving dinner at the table in the kitchen, seven of us squished in on folding chairs at the breakfast table, which was probably designed for four. Dean made a turducken, a chicken inside a duck inside a turkey. We had stuffing, green beans, and sweet potatoes, and I made a few pies. It was a nice night, pretty close to my fantasy of a cozy, messy family holiday.

My mother left without ever saying anything about the

house, and I suppose that was her way of being polite. But after she left I realized how much I'd wanted to hear that she was proud of me. Dean and I were leading a simple life, surrounded by our children and animals. We were cooking and doing everything ourselves. It was so different from how I'd grown up. Couldn't she see? I'd turned into a real homemaker!

The next day my mother forwarded me an e-mail that she'd sent to her best friend. Her friend had asked about Thanksgiving, and my mother's response was, "Let me tell you how great it was. They're living their dream. Their own *Green Acres*. A pig greeted me at the door. They cooked a fabulous dinner." The e-mail said everything I'd wanted her to say! She got it. I was a Beverly Hills girl who'd moved to a farm. (In Malibu, but still.) When I asked her if the e-mail was for me or for her friend, she said, "Both of you." She was being supportive in her own way. That was enough for me.

For Christmas we went to Lake Arrowhead, to a house that we were renting for the second year in a row with Patsy, the Guncles, Simone, and Scout's mother, Grandma Jacquie. It was a Tudor house right on the lake, with big open bay windows and a great gourmet kitchen with all Viking appliances. There were too many fake florals around the house for my taste, but the amazing huge fireplaces more than made up for that.

We went to a Christmas-tree lot and I decided to go for it—I bought an all-white flocked tree. We bought plastic ornaments and colored lights at CVS.

Usually it snows in Lake Arrowhead and we go skiing or sledding, but that year it was warmer. We didn't do much of anything. We'd go into the village to poke around, or stay home, walking the kids down to the lake to feed the ducks, watching movies, and cooking every single meal. It was a big house—unlike Malibu there was plenty of room for all of us—and was really restful. A brief reprieve before a surprising curveball.

Is There a Mall
in This Seaside Resort?

In the beginning of January 2012 we took a little trip to Pasadena for work. It was the up-fronts for *Tori & Dean*—the day when NBC affiliates presented their seasonal lineup to advertisers and press. The event was taking place at the iconic Langham hotel. Most people who were attending just drove in for the day, but since we lived so far away—in Malibu—they put us, the three kids, and Patsy up at the hotel for the night.

The night we arrived Dean and I were supposed to make an appearance at a red-carpet cocktail party. The next day was the press tour. Media outlets would have tables set up on the hotel's lawn, and celebrities from all of the NBC/Universal shows would make the rounds, doing interviews. Then we'd head home. It would be a condensed but important trip.

All that day I sensed it coming, and, indeed, by the time we arrived at the hotel I had developed a full-blown migraine. I was expected at the cocktail party downstairs. They'd paid for our suite and everything. The hair and makeup people were there, at the ready. But I couldn't function. This night was a big deal for us, our show, and our network. I was in tears, not knowing whether I should drag myself to the party and pretend to function or rest in hope of recovering so I could do press the next day. My publicist told me to rest—the next day was even more important—so I went straight to bed. I lay there with the lights out and an ice pack on my head. I did manage to eat some truffled Parmesan fries and to catch a few scenes from *Contagion* on pay-per-view.

The next morning, when I woke up, I couldn't see straight. I was weeping with pain. We had to cancel the whole press day. Dean and I were in some ways the faces of the network. We were Oxygen's most recognizable show, and one of their top shows. This was really, really bad.

I needed to go to the ER, but how? There was press everywhere. We would certainly be followed. Dean called down to the front desk to ask if there was a way we could leave without being seen. Security guards led us down through the kitchen and out a back way. We slipped into the hotel shuttle, and the driver dropped us off at the ER.

A nurse brought me to a room. Before taking my vitals, she handed me a cup.

"Before we can treat you, we have to make sure you're not pregnant."

This was not my first time at the races. For my worst migraines, one or two times a year, I end up in the hospital. I'd never been asked to pee for pain meds before.

I whispered to the nurse, "Oh no, my baby is only two months old. There's not a shot in hell I'm pregnant. I've been a migraine sufferer my whole life. It's fine to treat me."

But the nurse wanted the pee, and I wanted the headache to subside, so I complied.

I FELT LIKE a character in *Days of Our Lives*, suffering from my fiftieth brain tumor, the one that would surely be my demise. I lay in the darkness of a hospital room, an ice pack on my forehead, murmuring, "Where's the doctor? I just need the pain meds . . ."

An older man with white hair came into the room. My chart was hanging on a clipboard at the foot of the bed. He looked down at the clipboard.

"Mrs. McDermott? I just want to let you know . . ." he said.

"Yes?"

"That you're . . . you're pregnant."

IT WAS LIKE an out-of-body experience. I remember thinking, *Wow, this is what it's like to be really shocked by something.* Like a surprise party. Or like finding out you've been left 0.16 percent of your gazillionaire father's estate. (Love him. Still bitter.)

I looked at Dean. He looked back at me. Oh. My. God.

"That's not possible," I told the doctor.

"The test shows that you're pregnant," he said.

"You don't understand. I just gave birth!"

The doctor looked at me with mild impatience. I could see that he thought I was crazy, but I still needed him to understand that he was wrong.

"We could do a blood test," he said. "The blood test will tell us definitively."

"Yes, please," I said. "You'll see." The blood test might not have a little window with words saying "not pregnant," but I knew it would prove me right. I was sure it would be conclusive.

They took blood. The thirty minutes we waited for the results passed like an eternity. My head pounded like I was the cartoon Tom, and Jerry had just crashed my head between two enormous cymbals.

Finally the doctor returned. "Well, you're definitely pregnant."

"I'm so confused," I said. "Tell me how this happened."

He just looked at me.

"We only had sex once!" I said. Oh. We only had sex once. Or twice.

THEN, AS IF I wasn't already reeling with this news, the doctor said, "Because you're pregnant, we cannot treat you."

No!

I thought back to when I'd been pregnant with Hattie. I'd had a migraine at the very beginning then too, before Dean even knew I was pregnant. The ER near our house had treated me that time. But this conservative doctor wouldn't do it.

I texted my obstetrician, Dr. J. He wasn't going to be happy with me. The pack of nursing-mom-appropriate birth-control pills he'd prescribed for me were lost somewhere in our house. Months later, Dean would discover them nestled in a toolbox in the garage. We're still confused as to how they ended up there. I don't use tools.

Dr. J was flummoxed at this news, but he got on the

phone with the doctor and told him it was okay to administer pain medication. Afterward, we texted and Dr. J said, "Take your time. Digest this news. I want you to know that I totally support you whatever you want to do."

I was horrified. Terminating the pregnancy was not an option for me. Did I want to be pregnant right now? No. Did I want another baby? Not so soon! But there was no way I was going to mess with fate.

The nurses left to get my medicine, and for the first time Dean and I were alone with our embryo and my pounding head. Dean said, "This is another blessing."

They finally gave me the pain medication. I lay there for hours, waiting for the pain to fade, processing what was happening. I felt like I'd just come back from outer space and was being sent back up in a rocket the next day. Oh my God, I was embarking on this journey again. I was scared. Hattie was only two months old, and I was already one month pregnant. I was still nursing the baby. People were still congratulating me on the birth. I hadn't even begun to think about losing the weight. But I was bouncing back pretty well. I felt great (other than this migraine). This baby was meant to be.

AFTER THE DISASTROUS up-fronts, back in Malibu, we weren't exactly settling into life on the farm. I had pushed so hard to move to the house, and one weekend later I knew we'd made a huge mistake. Now we were expecting a fourth child. We already had Patsy and Hattie in one bedroom, and Liam and Stella, plus Jack every other weekend, in the other. Where would the new baby go? In the trailer? Under a tarp outside with all the still-packed boxes? But we had just moved. We couldn't admit defeat . . . yet.

Aside from the space, we weren't exactly fitting into the community. I couldn't figure out the Malibu women. They wore Uggs and sweatpants with Cartier bracelets and diamond-faced Rolexes. They wore six-carat engagement rings alongside woven friendship bracelets with a made-with-their-kids look. They were super casual, their professionally sun-kissed hair thrown up in messy buns as if they didn't care. Their cozy, washed-a-million-times, perfectly worn sweatshirts were from Free City and cost two hundred dollars. And they were universally tall, blond, and tan, with great bodies and so much plastic surgery that I couldn't tell if one was thirty, forty, or fifty. They were basically the beachy version of Beverly Hills trophy wives. Here in the 'Bu, instead of shopping, getting Botox, and drinking cabernet in the afternoon, they walked on the beach every day, did yoga, and drank green drinks. Beverly Hills had its high-fashion moms who wore blazers and jeans, diamond necklaces, and heels or designer flats. A Malibu woman wouldn't be caught dead wearing a blazer. But they were all the same to me. It was winter and my summer fling with Malibu was so over.

And it's not like Malibu was knocking on my door, wanting to be best friends. Our first week in the house, we had filmed *Tori & Dean* for one day, shooting the final scenes of the season, and, although we didn't know it at the time, of the show. When the show premiered, Oxygen came to our house and had live cuts of the family watching the premiere in Malibu. That night there was a truck parked in front of our house, with a satellite with a live feed.

Late that night I was in the kitchen, wearing a tank top and underwear, getting myself a glass of sparkling water with lemon. A man I'd never seen before opened our wooden gate and walked toward the kitchen's sliding door. I'm a girl who, when house-hunting at age twenty-six, assumed the place I lived would have a guard's room because I thought that everyone had guards on staff, in need of their own rooms. I screamed, "Dean! Dean! There's a man coming to the door. I don't know what he wants!"

Dean came out from the bedroom and went into the front yard to talk to the stranger. I listened from inside.

The stranger launched into an angry tirade. He said, "I'm your neighbor from across the street. So I don't know

who you people are, but my kid says you do some sort of
TV show. You're filming here. I don't know what you're
doing. We're not like that here in Point Dume. We don't
have people like that here."

I flashed back to the neighbor we'd had way back when
we'd lived on Beaver Avenue. He'd seen our cameras and
said, "You might be making porns in there."

Our Malibu neighbor went on with his disjointed tirade. "Everyone knows everyone. The lights from your
truck were on. My kid couldn't sleep. I'm having a Christmas party next week. Everyone comes to it. I'm sure you'd
like to bring your wife to it. It's the party of the year. But
we're not like that here in Point Dume."

His tone was bullying. He was right in Dean's face,
pointing his finger right at him.

Dean said, "Get your finger out of my face."

Then our new neighbor got pissed off. "Oh, you're
going to be like that? I see how you people are. You know
what? On second thought, we don't want your types at
our party. You're not invited to our party."

The neighbor stalked away. Dean came back in. "Welcome to the neighborhood," he said.

When my friend Madison heard that we weren't adjust-
ing to Malibu, he decided to help us out. Madison is one
of the real estate agents on the Bravo show *Million Dollar Listing*. He is young and handsome and perpetually

tan. We'd become friends through my production company, and he was the one who'd helped us get our summer
rental next to Kelly Wearstler. He hadn't found our current house for us—when he saw it he said he would have
talked us out of it. We text all the time, and when I expressed doubts about Malibu, he said, "Don't worry. I'm
going to show you around. Malibu is a pocket of heaven."
According to Madison, we just had to get to know the
right people. There were great families, but we had to
know how to navigate. I became Madison's pet project.
He would help me come to love Malibu.

Madison really wanted me to meet all his favorite Malibu girls, and he said the best way was to take a certain
dance class in the upscale Malibu Lumber Yard, a shopping complex adjacent to Malibu Country Mart that was
a former lumberyard. I don't go in much for group activities, much less any form of exercise, but I finally dragged
my postpartum, pregnant self to this dance class.

It was a super-fast-paced class. Like Zumba, I think, although I'm not fully up to speed on workout-class trends.
I was miserably out of shape. My pregnancy was still a
secret (this again!), so I told the teacher that I was trying
to lose the baby weight, but I was actually worried that all
this jumping around was going to shake the embryo loose
(which would turn out to be a much more real concern
than I knew).

The teacher was good at what she did. And Madison had clearly suggested that she play friend-matchmaker for me. After class, when we were chatting, she said, "You know Alecia, right?" No, I didn't know Alecia.

"You know . . . Pink? I should introduce you to her. You guys would really hit it off." I didn't know Pink. I don't have many celebrity friends. I'm friends with Jenny from the west side. But the teacher clearly thought that my best options for new friends were other celebrities. She threw some other celebrity-mom names at me. She said, "Brooke. Minnie. They all come here. I get them back into shape."

Of all the celebrity moms she knew, she was most enthusiastic about Pink for me. I tried to imagine the two of us bombing down Cross Creek Road together, pushing strollers. Hmm. Our husbands did both have tattoos. I couldn't really see it, but I do love her song "Just Like a Pill."

Madison so wanted me to love Malibu, but instead I missed Encino, of all places. I had thought the streets in Encino were ugly. I'd bitched about our Valley life. Now I longed for the frozen yogurt on every corner, the karate, dance, and princess classes for the kids. Where were Malibu's family-friendly chain restaurants—the Buca di Beppo, the Chili's? Where were the cheap Chinese nail salons? Stella and I liked to get Minx Nails, which are like fun stickers that decorate fingernails. At CVS the Sally Hansen knockoff ones are maybe ten dollars for a set. But at the one and only nail salon that finally opened in Malibu, some Zen décor and foot bowls later, the cute, silly mother-daughter Minx Nails excursion cost a total of three hundred dollars!

Malibu is a very small town. It has its own retro-chic vibe: farmers from the seventies living next to mansions with film producers and their trophy wives. The Malibu Country Mart and Lumber Yard had some of my favorite stores—Intermix, Alice + Olivia, Planet Blue. I thought I'd be happy walking around those boutiques. But who was I kidding? I couldn't afford to shop there all the time anyway. And because there was only one area to shop, it was riddled with paparazzi. There was nothing for our family to do. We were pretty much isolated at home.

We soon found ourselves driving to the Valley, to the very area we'd left. We'd spend a Saturday at the Topanga mall, shopping, eating in the food court, and scrambling around the indoor playground. I couldn't help thinking, *I used to live ten minutes from this mall.*

What possessed me? What made me think it was okay to move from a six-thousand-square-foot house to a two-thousand-square-foot house . . . with a baby on the way? I know I was swayed by the acreage. The chickens would have a huge coop. Hank the pig would love it. But why didn't I spend more time thinking about where my children would sleep? When it came down to it, we hadn't bought a house where we could live. It was a what-if house. An if-we-had-another-million-dollars house. I'd spent all my time fantasizing about tending to my chickens in a painted coop with a chandelier hanging inside. I hadn't taken the time to think about whether we'd be happy there in the interim—before we could make all the changes I envisioned. To be honest, all I really asked the Realtor was whether the house was haunted. I didn't want to live in a place where someone had died.

I thought back to the single time we'd met the former owners of the house. The Realtor had told us they were downsizing. They'd raised two kids here, picking blackberries in the backyard, and now for financial reasons needed something smaller. We were already in escrow, but we'd come to see the house one more time. The owners were already starting to move their stuff.

"Where are you moving?" I asked the woman.

"We're moving to a house off Mulholland. It's an extensive property, and we're having trouble with the contractor who's building it."

This whole notion of downsizing was a lie. They weren't downsizing. They were upgrading. The house was a money pit.

I wanted a farmhouse—but one that was completely

updated with gleaming hardwood floors and modern appliances. I wanted a flower bed and a garden. I was having such a nice summer at our rental house in Malibu that I wanted that to be my life. But even that house was over three thousand square feet! My friends, including Jenny, claim I didn't show them the house until I'd already bought it.

Sometimes I think I got lost in the madness of the reality show. The producer in me thought, *What a great story line! All of us crowded in a small house, roughing it until we have the money to expand. We could do this, and we could film it too!* Producers want conflict. But this was my real life. Why had I brought this on myself? I didn't want to live a life of self-inflicted contrived conflict!

Or did this go beyond the reality madness? Why couldn't I settle down in a home? What was I searching for?

At the same time as I asked myself these questions, I thought about the space, and baby number four, and what lay ahead. No matter how fickle I was about my real estate decisions, this time we really had to move. We had to move.

This time it wasn't an exciting prospect. It was an overwhelming problem. We'd bought the house in Malibu before we sold our house in Encino. We'd ended up selling Encino at a loss. A big loss. We couldn't afford to buy another house.

Song and Dance

I was panicked about wanting to move, having the new baby, and being able to afford all of it. Whenever I panic about money, I spring into action. We found out I was pregnant the first week of January. I quickly landed two jobs that were both supposed to start right away, at the same time in different cities, but after some rescheduling it was all set: The first week of February I would film a Christmas TV movie for ABC Family. It was called *The Mistle-Tones*, and it was shooting in Utah. The minute I returned, I'd start filming a new reality competition series, *Craft Wars*, for TLC. When it rains it pours. I didn't mention to either job that I was pregnant. It was still too early—we had heard the heartbeat and my doctor said that everything looked good, but what if something went wrong? I was worried about taking on so much work with two kids, a newborn, and a secret pregnancy. But if I wanted to find us a way out of Malibu in time for baby number four, I'd have to work my ass off throughout the pregnancy.

When I was first offered the role of Marci in *The Mistle-Tones*, my reaction was: *A Christmas movie of the week—cool!* In the nineties, movies of the week had been my bread and butter (*Mother, May I Sleep with Danger?* anyone?). As I skimmed the script I grew confused. Wait a minute, the lead character was Holly! Who was Marci? I flipped back through the script. Oh. Marci was the second lead. I was bummed. I used to be the star of the screen for two hours. Now I was playing second fiddle. This was where my life had gone. And my character was very one-note—a bitchy, territorial leader of a singing group. I had a call with the writers. Could Marci be campy and snarky but also get in her own way? So she wasn't just a straight-on bitch? The writers were on board with making her a bit more dimensional, so I felt better about it.

In the beginning, the producers asked if I could sing. Through my agent, I told them that I'd done a little singing in movies, but not much. They said not to worry—I had maybe one line in a Christmas song, like "walking in a winter wonderland" or something like that. That was my only solo.

Next thing I knew, I was told to meet with a voice coach in L.A., Eric Vetro. This voice coach was *the* guy. Voice coach to the stars. Yikes. As soon as Eric Vetro heard me sing one note, he'd surely send me packing. But as I sat waiting outside his music room, I heard his prior appointment working with him in the other room. It was some actress singing horribly off-key. I heard him say, "Okay, that's great." That made me feel better. I heard him say good-bye, and then the actress walked out of the room. It was Katie Holmes.

I'd met Katie Holmes years ago, in her *Dawson's Creek* days, when I was still on *90210*. A friend of mine at the time did a movie with her, *Teaching Mrs. Tingle*. One night he said, "Can I bring Katie from my movie out to drinks?" We went to Trader Vic's, which was my go-to hang at the time. We ordered the Scorpion Bowl, their signature drink, which was served in a big white Hawaiian bowl with a bunch of straws for sharing. It was kind of gross when you thought about it. We were all swapping spit. But at least the alcohol killed the germs. *Dawson's Creek* Katie was exactly what you'd expect. She was wearing jeans and a tank top. Her hair was down. She was shy but engaging, and altogether pretty adorable. It was a long time ago, but I remembered the night pretty well. She must have remembered too.

"Hi, how are you?" she said.

I said, "Oh, hi!" I didn't know whether we should hug or shake hands. But the signal from her was immediately clear: Don't even come close. I instantly got nervous. We clearly weren't going to catch up on the last ten years. And we certainly weren't going to talk about her husband, Tom Cruise. (I had a *Top Gun* poster of him in my room growing up, just like she did.) When all else fails, I always pull out the mommy card. It breaks the tension. "Your daughter is adorable. I have kids around the same age."

"Oh, do you?" she said.

Then I was annoyed. Come on. Okay, I know you're busy. But you're in the public eye. Don't tell me you don't follow the tabloids. Don't tell me you don't know anything about other celebrities and their kids.

"Yes, my son is almost five. My daughter's almost four, and I just had a baby."

She said, "Oh? Congratulations." Then we stood there. She was just plastic. In a perfectly polite way.

"Well, good to see you," I said. She went out to her car, and her driver whisked her away.

I was sweating. My pits were drenched. I never sweat. It was that awkward. I thought, *I know you're not a robot be-*

cause you can't sing for shit. (Oh my God, I'm a mean person.) As my anxiety faded, I just felt sorry for her. I hadn't expected her to reminisce, but this was a totally different person from the girl I'd met at Trader Vic's. I felt sad for her. Those paparazzi photos, the ones where she looks like she's miserable but putting on a happy face? That's what she looked like in person. Not long after that encounter, the news would break that she and Tom had split up.

Now it was my turn to meet with Eric Vetro. When I walked in and we met, he said, "Actually, we met once before. I came to your mom's Christmas party. I was Sean Hayes's plus-one." Me, Katie, Eric, Sean, Candy. Such a small world.

His studio walls were covered with records. There were pictures of every celebrity. If they could sing, or be made to sing, then so could I . . . right? The producers had sent a tape with the music I was supposed to sing. Eric played it for me. It was a whole song, start to finish. I was singing solo. And this wasn't good old "Jingle Bells." It was Mariah Carey's "All I Want for Christmas Is You" and the person singing it on the demo was way out of my league.

The voice coach said, "They're going for a *Glee* sound with the song." As if that was at all useful to me. It just made it all the more scary.

"I can't sing like that," I told the voice coach. "I can sing cute! But I can't belt out notes. And I just had a baby!

I don't have the air." I was going to work this newborn thing for as long as I could. The truth was, whatever it was that one might do to work one's diaphragm, I hadn't done it in years. Unless it was covered in the Malibu dance class I did that one time.

"Let's just try," he said. "Don't worry. The worst that happens is that they bring a professional singer in."

I apologized a million times, and he could see how worried I was.

"Let me get you some Throat Coat tea," he said. "It helps relax your vocal cords."

But before he could get the tea, he took a business call. Then he left the room, and when he came back, he didn't have any tea. I was too shy to mention it, so I just took a sip from my water bottle.

He said, "Let's practice scales."

I sang a scale. "That was terrible!" I moaned.

"Stop doubting yourself. Let's do the song line by line. We'll ease into it."

I started the song. It was not going well.

He said, "Take a sip of your Throat Coat tea."

But I didn't have the tea. He'd never gotten me any. I smiled and took a sip of my water, hoping he'd forget about it.

"No, try the tea," he said.

"No, I'm okay," I said.

He reached over to a table beside me and picked up a Styrofoam cup. "Take a sip," he said.

He was holding the cup right up to my face. It was almost empty. He was being insistent and I was so mortified that I couldn't bring myself to say, "This is Katie Holmes's cold backwash of Throat Coat tea."

I drank it. As he watched, I downed Katie Holmes's backwash. It was gross and creepy and definitely unsanitary. Sure, we'd swapped spit years ago with the Scorpion Bowl, but that had germ-killing alcohol! It was disgusting, but in some weird universe, it was better than drinking a stranger's tea. At least she was an A-lister. Or married to one.

By the end of our session Eric had me record the whole song. I could hear that it was off, but not bad for my first time singing in years. He told me that if we had weeks to work on it, we could probably get it to a place where I was comfortable, but since we only had one session, he was going to recommend that they bring in someone to mix with my voice and enhance it. I was fine with that!

A few days later I went to a recording session. I recorded the song, and then a cute professional singer in her thirties sang along with my recording. I heard her do it. She had a soulful, raspy voice. I have a white-girl cutesy voice. They had her do it again with a more pop-y feel. Of course she could do that—she could do anything.

This girl was known for matching different singers' voices. She'd done Beyoncé, Britney Spears, Jennifer Lopez. In theory, her voice would blend with mine, enhancing the places I couldn't hit.

I didn't hear the song until I was on set and had to mouth it. I was aghast. It was probably 95 percent professional singer and 5 percent me. At best. I could barely recognize myself until it came to the last "All I want for Christmas is you." The very last word of the song was me. And one "baby" somewhere in there. Ah well, I never said I could sing.

TWO DAYS BEFORE the whole family left for Utah, I got a massage at home in Malibu. I was eight weeks pregnant. My friend Cheyenne, who used to do massages for us (and, let's not forget, the fabulous Kelly Wearstler), had been on maternity leave for a while, and since Hattie was four months old I'd been working with a male masseuse whom Cheyenne had suggested. When she first recommended Brendan, I asked if he was gay. She said she couldn't divulge that information, but that the two of us would get along. From that, I was confident that he was straight-friendly. I hadn't known him long, but I was semicomfortable with him. Still, I didn't tell him I was pregnant. I wasn't telling anyone yet, and it was early enough that I could still lie on my stomach and not worry about it.

I lay down on the table on my stomach. Brendan had barely started when I coughed. I felt something wet—had I peed a little? How weird and embarrassing. Maybe this was what happened in a fourth pregnancy. Anyway, Brendan started working on my shoulders, and I felt more wetness. This was getting awkward. I hoped the pee wasn't visible or anything. Then Brendan paused to get a sip of water and I reached down to the wetness. I looked at my hand and freaked when I realized it was blood. I rolled over and looked down at myself. There was blood everywhere. A lot of blood. My heart dropped. My fingertips went numb. I screamed, "Oh my God! I'm so sorry. I have to get up. I'm pregnant. And I'm bleeding. I think I'm having a miscarriage. I'm so sorry, oh, I don't know what to do."

I climbed off the table and headed to the bathroom, yelling for Dean. By the time I cleaned myself up, it seemed that the bleeding had stopped. But I had no idea what it meant. Had I miscarried? I texted Dr. J and sent him a picture of the blood.

He texted me back, *"take it easy. if it's a miscarriage, there's nothing you can do to stop it. it'll have to run its course. come in tomorrow, first thing."*

While Brendan packed up, I apologized to him about his sheets.

Brendan, trying to make light of the moment, gasped, "Oh no, my best Martha Stewart sheets!" I laughed. He speculated that he could get some good money for the Tori-tainted sheets on eBay. We decided we would split the profit: his sheets, my blood.

Brendan and I were joking around, but that night I was distraught. What had gone wrong? By the next day, when Dean and I went in to Dr. J for an ultrasound, I was shaking. As Dr. J put the gel on, I braced myself for the worst news.

"What do you see? What do you see?" I said.

"You mean this heartbeat? This perfectly normal heartbeat? Your baby's fine."

Dr. J thought the bleeding could have been a cyst that expelled itself, but whatever it was, I had nothing to worry about. These things happened. The baby had grown, it was moving, its heartbeat was normal, we were fine.

We left for Utah the next day.

APPARENTLY, IN ADDITION to the singing, the *Mistle-Tones* producers hadn't noticed that there was no danc-ing on my résumé. I didn't even think about the dancing until I got to Utah. In hindsight, there had been some warning. They had asked me to fly to Utah a week early for dance rehearsals. Dance rehearsals? Hadn't I read the script right? It was about a Christmas singing group. The singing was enough of a challenge, but what kind of dancing would I be doing? Anyway, I couldn't come early—I was doing pre-prep for *Craft Wars*, my upcoming reality show. So when I arrived in Utah I was dismayed to see that they had me scheduled for *six hours* of dance a day. First the singing, now this? Had my agent pitched me as a triple threat? I hadn't worked out in years. In fact, the only time I'd worked out in the last three years was the Zumba-like class I did with the Malibu moms where the teacher tried to push Pink on me. Plus I was pregnant. I had bled on a massage table. I was terrified of moving.

My first day in Utah I showed up at the six-hour dance rehearsal, where I was introduced to two dance pieces choreographed by Danny Teeson, a big-time choreographer. That was when I found out that everyone else who had been hired to be in my singing group in the movie was a professional dancer. Some may have had a little acting experience, but they didn't have many lines. The girl who played my best friend was a local hire, an actress from Utah, but even she had a singing and dancing background. I'd never even been asked if I had rhythm!

At the end of that first day I was so exhausted I couldn't stand. But I went straight from there to a wardrobe fitting. My costumes were all sparkly, skintight gowns. I had to wear two pairs of Spanx. I felt self-conscious and big. I still had a jiggly Hattie belly—I was only three months out—and another pregnancy coming up behind it!

My character, Marci, was fun and bitchy but still a little one-note for my taste. Luckily, the director gave me some freedom to play with the part. Overall, it was such a nice set and such a fun experience. It really made me want to be acting again.

WHEN I WAS making *The Mistle-Tones*, I fell in love with Salt Lake City. There was beautiful farmland, gorgeous houses. The food was good, the people were nice. They even had vintage shops. I started thinking . . . *Maybe we should move to Utah*. It was only an hour and a half by plane from L.A. At first, it was just a fantasy, the same basic fantasy I have whenever we travel. But soon the fantasy wove into real life. I couldn't go back to Malibu. We had to move. Not to Salt Lake City, but to a place that made sense for our growing family. I knew we were in the hole and that if we moved again, we'd have to rent. So at night, after finishing the day's work on *The Mistle-Tones*, I took to the web.

Then I found the perfect place. It was a spacious house in a gated community in Westlake Village, about an hour from L.A. I'd always longed for the privacy of a gated community. This one was surrounded by mountains. There was a lake, plenty of bedrooms, hardwood floors, a screening room. I showed it to Dean, and he got excited, but then I told him the price. We couldn't afford it. It cost twice what our business manager said we could spend. But I wanted to try. It had been on the market for a year. Maybe if we pulled on their heartstrings they'd come down in price. Maybe they wanted a nice family as tenants. I decided not to mention the chickens and goats. And the pig.

MEANWHILE, I NEVER stopped spotting and cramping. Dr. J had to be wrong. I was miscarrying. Or if I hadn't been before, I was now, after all that dancing. I started convincing myself that I wasn't pregnant anymore. I was three months pregnant and I hadn't even popped yet. When I texted Dr. J, he said, "*If you're really concerned, go to local ER and have them examine you.*"

There was no way I was going to the local ER. Instead, I spent the month in Utah convinced I had a dead baby inside of me.

I WANTED TO see Dr. J the minute we got back to Los Angeles, but I had to do a session of jewelry hawking for

HSN first. (I love my jewelry and I love what I do, but there are only so many ways to say, "Please buy my product," on TV.) There were several more days of traveling and stewing before I could have an appointment. By the time I got to Dr. J's office, I was a nervous wreck. As soon as a nurse led me into the examining room, I burst into tears.

"What's wrong?" the nurse asked.

"I'm so sure I had a miscarriage," I said. "I'm not even showing."

She asked for my urine sample and said she'd test my levels right away. Moments later, she came back to my room.

"What does it show?" I asked.

"It's pretty low," she said. I began to sob. She hurried out of the room to get the doctor.

When Dr. J came in, he said, "You know, your levels are normal. They drop down at this point in the pregnancy."

I said, "I had a dream that I came in to see you. You said, 'It's gonna be okay, don't worry.' You turned to look at the ultrasound monitor, and then looked back at me and said, 'I'm sorry.'"

He said, "Stop writing the movie in your head. Let's take a look."

While he started the ultrasound, I was crying hysterically. I couldn't look at Dr. J. Everything was happening as I'd seen it in my dream. He was consoling me. Dean was standing on the other side. I knew the face Dr. J was going to give me next—it would be a look of the same sympathetic sorrow I had seen in my dream.

Then he turned to me with a big smile. "Healthy baby! I keep telling you."

EVERYTHING WAS FINE. I went home that night, and the next morning when I woke up, I had a full, round, hard belly. My fear had somehow held my belly back. I know it sounds crazy, but when I showed Dean, he said, "Babe! You have a huge belly!"

At that moment it became real to me. The baby was okay. I was really, truly pregnant.

Now that our fourth child was a certainty, we just had to move. It became an obsession. We went to look at the fantasy house in Westlake Village. We met the owners, who seemed to like us. I had to get the house. I had to win! We confided in them that we were expecting a fourth and how much the house meant to us. They came down a bit, but the rent was still obscene. Nonetheless, we took it. And we still hadn't sold Malibu.

Doing belly shots—kids kiss the baby not knowing if it's a boy or a girl (soon-to-be Hattie).

My gusband, Mehran, and I have a much-needed girlfriend day! Here we are watching our last movie before Hattie was born the next day.

Stella hugging her cousin Simone at the baby shower for baby Hattie.

Me in my DIY hospital gown with my three babes, currently unaware that one month from this photo I'd be preggers again!

Courtesy of Dean McDermott

My first moment wit newborn Hattie— one reality moment I wish had been priva

Courtesy of Mario Panagiotopoulos

Liam cuddles with baby sister Hattie.

Courtesy of Dean McDerr

Just a normal day in the McDermott household. . . .
What? Not everyone has a pig peeking in their fridge?

Our whole gang!

My chicken, Coco, reminds me so
much of my pug, Mimi La Rue.
She even loves to wear clothing!
FashionablePoultry

Hattie's first time in the pool.
One milestone that was
all her and me.

Stella giving her new cousin Simone a welcome-to-the-family kiss! #GunclesBabe

Hattie sporting Mom's shades. #InfantChic

Loved our Christmas vacations at Lake Arrowhead with our family and the Guncles' family.

Filming my ABC Family Christmas movie, *The Mistle-Tones.* No one knew I was hiding this scary early pregnancy, so I was wearing two pairs of Spanx and trying my best to keep up with all the singing and dancing.

Putting my best pose on after I just had a major bleed when pregnant with Finn. After this pic, I went straight to the doctor and then on bed rest. #TheShowMustGoOn

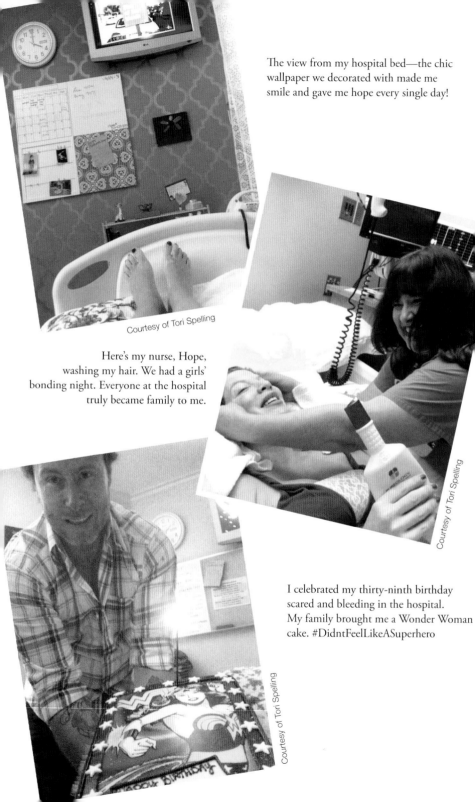

The view from my hospital bed—the chic wallpaper we decorated with made me smile and gave me hope every single day!

Here's my nurse, Hope, washing my hair. We had a girls' bonding night. Everyone at the hospital truly became family to me.

I celebrated my thirty-ninth birthday scared and bleeding in the hospital. My family brought me a Wonder Woman cake. #DidntFeelLikeASuperhero

(Top left, clockwise) (1) Liam graduating from preschool. I waited three years for that moment, spent months choosing the perfect outfit for him, and sadly had to watch it via FaceTime from my hospital bed. (2) My amazing family sent me pictures like this daily to lift my spirits while in the hospital. (3) Stella waving to me from her fourth birthday party, which I also missed because I was hospital-bound. #MomentsICantGetBack (4) Departure day—saying good-bye to the hospital, aka my second home, after two and a half months. Hardest, darkest, yet most eye-opening experience of my life. #MomWarrior

(All photos courtesy of Dean McDermott)

My first moment holding baby Finn. I softly whispered in his ear, "We made it!"

Courtesy of ElizabethMessina.com

Courtesy of Tori Spelling

Mommy and Finn. Still in awe of the journey we took together.

Finn's first family shower. Loved it so much he fell asleep. #CozyFamilyTime

Courtesy of Tori Spelling

Martha Moments

*C*raft Wars was my next project. It had come about after Dean and I had wrapped sTORIbook Weddings and when celebraTORI, my party-planning book, was about to come out. I went to TLC with a pitch book showing everything I love: the wedding planning, the parties, the crafting, the cooking, my blog. I was starting to think of myself as kind of a modern, imperfect, girl-friend-y, and of course fashion-forward Martha Stewart. With some debt but a clean record.

I had actually met Martha Stewart back in September 2010. Martha was to me what Madonna is to Mehran: Iconic. My inspiration. The one person I'd always wanted to meet. When my children's book, *Presenting . . . Tallulah*, came out I asked my publicist if she could summon all her powers to help me meet Martha. She did it! She landed me a visit to the show to promote the book and do kids' crafts with Martha herself.

My appearance on *Martha* was scheduled for September 21, which happens to be the birthday of my biggest fan. The first time I met Darren Martin was at a book signing at Bookends in New Jersey. He'd driven fourteen hours from New Brunswick, Canada, to be there. Ever since then we've kept in touch via Twitter, and he shows up at lots of my events. I'm grateful for his dedication, and I always try to move him to the front of the line and to take pictures with him. When Darren heard I was going to be on *Martha*, he told me he was coming to town for his birthday. It happened to coincide with the show and he was hoping to get tickets, but it looked like the show was sold out. I invited him to come backstage and hang out while I was getting ready. Darren said that it was going to be the coolest moment ever, watching his idol (me!) meet her idol (Martha!).

When the show started, I was backstage with Darren, Mehran, and my publicist. I wanted to make a good impression on Martha, and I was worried that my voice would crack, or anything else might happen to make the moment less than perfect. My fantasy was basically the same as that of me and Kelly Wearstler, but substituting crafting for design: She'd meet me and think, *Wow, Tori really can craft. She's cool. She can hang out with me.*

I walked out onstage and the first thing Martha said to me was, "You're going to craft in those heels?"

I said, "What? Martha, doesn't everyone craft in Louboutins?" I thought it was worth a chuckle but got nothin'.

Martha and I were making adorable papier-mâché hot-air balloons to hang in the kids' rooms. Everything had been prepped for us to make sure we could complete the craft during the allocated segment. But at some point we came to a part where she and I were both supposed to cut strips of tape. She had a roll of thin tape on her side of the table, but mine was nowhere to be seen. She handled this minor oversight perfectly calmly while we were on the air, but then we went to break. She stood next to me, not talking to me or making eye contact, just standing there next to me. Staff rushed in, and she said, "Where was her tape? We couldn't do the project properly." She didn't raise her voice, but the tone was not nice. I got it. In a heartbeat, I got exactly what type of person she was. Me and Martha, our crafting-buddy future—it wasn't happening.

Before we'd even begun, I'd told my publicist I really wanted a picture of me and Martha. When we were done, Martha started to leave, but my publicist stepped up and asked about a picture.

"Only if it looks organic," Martha said. She handed me my hot-air balloon and took hers in hand. I looked up at the camera, smiling, and Martha looked down at the balloon, as if she were working on it. Organic. My publicist took the picture. Then Martha put down her craft and walked offstage without so much as a glance in my direction. We were done. I was horrified. I thought about how when I did Rachael Ray, she was all about girl power. She was like, "Oh, you wrote this book? Good for you. Let's tell the world." We made my cupcake cones together. When we went to commercial, we chatted. It was all very pleasant. I'd expected at least the same from Martha. Sure, I'd heard rumors about her, but I had still put her on a pedestal. I came on her show not just as a celebrity but as a true fan. Our long-awaited encounter was my *Wizard of Oz* moment. I'd seen behind the curtain. As for the papier-mâché balloons we'd crafted "for my kids"? Her staff promised to send them to me, but I never saw them again.

Back in the greenroom, Darren was on cloud nine. He was so happy and proud. "This is such a great day," he said. I couldn't burst his bubble. (Or his papier-mâché balloon.) But I was so bummed.

AFTER MY DISAPPOINTING encounter with Martha, my desire to be the new, modern Martha Stewart surged.

Who could relate to this woman? Sure, her work was great. But people want projects they can actually execute. They want to connect with the host. They want to know it's okay to make mistakes. I burn things. I spill things. But then I find ways to recover and make it work. Martha Stewart, with her cold, relentless perfection, is a dying breed. Who wants that? Especially in a show about the *hearth*, for God's sake! When I went to pitch at TLC, I was hoping (like many others, I'm sure) to create a show that would jump-start my "move over, Martha" campaign.

I told TLC that I wanted to do a broad lifestyle show. I cook, I bake, I decorate, I build, I craft, I design. And I love talking with women about all that. And relationships and mothering. I had the broad idea that I could do a show called something like *At Home with Tori*, where we did different segments in different rooms of my house. (Except not in Malibu, where I was living when I went in for the meeting. A single cameraman could hardly have fit in Malibu.)

TLC seemed particularly interested in my crafting. They were obsessed with a turkey costume I'd made for Hattie for Halloween and posted on my blog, *ediTORIal*. They came back to us saying that they were already developing a crafting show and that they thought I'd be the perfect host. *Craft Wars*, as it was to be called, would be produced by Super Delicious, the same company that did *Cupcake Wars* for the Food Network.

I told them that I didn't want to be a competition-show host like Ryan Seacrest on *Idol*. I wanted them to know how closely I worked with World of Wonder on *Tori & Dean*. I wasn't just an executive producer in name. I was hands-on. I had lots of ideas for how the show could work. TLC made it clear up front that the show was already pretty developed, so I asked to meet with Super Delicious to make sure my "executive producer" title wasn't a vanity thing.

"I want to be in the room with you developing the ideas, picking contestants, consulting on wardrobe." Everyone was excited and told me that yes, that was what they wanted too.

NOW, IMMEDIATELY AFTER we returned from shooting *The Mistle-Tones* in Utah, I started shooting on *Craft Wars*.

My belly was a problem. Someone had taken a picture of me when I was out shopping, and I'd instinctively put my purse in front of me. The universal celebrity pregnancy walk. The purse-block picture had run in the tabloids with "Is she pregnant again?" scrawled over it. It was still too early to go public with the pregnancy. Instead, I bemoaned the gossip to my stylist, Seth.

"Ugh. I still look huge!" I said. "People are going to think I'm pregnant."

"Please. Who would be that fucking crazy to get pregnant so soon after having a baby? Give me a break," Seth said.

I was like, *Yeah, who would be that crazy?*

This went on for a while, with me grilling him about whether he thought the producers would think I was pregnant and him saying, "Of course not. It's ridiculous. If they say one word about your weight, I'll remind them: you *just* had a baby." He was my biggest supporter.

I always wanted to keep my pregnancies secret for as long as possible, but this pregnancy felt like even more of a fragile, personal condition. I was on pins and needles because of the bleeding. Even though I was told everything was fine, I was superstitious that if I announced it something would go wrong. Now rumors were circulating. Finally, Meghan, my publicist, said, "Everyone thinks you're pregnant. We need to break the news. Better you announce it than they." I knew her thinking: By announcing, we would put an end to all the speculation.

First I had to tell Seth the truth. It was the day before we started filming. I said, "Seth, I have to tell you something. I'm pregnant."

He said, "Ha. Okay."

I said, "No, really. I'm three months pregnant."

"Shut the fuck up."

AROUND THIS TIME, Dean and I broke the news to Stella and Liam. I had a feeling they were going to respond well. I hadn't forgotten Liam's recent response when a mom at school had asked him about Hattie. She was three months old and they had taken a bath together for the first time. Hattie had a diaper rash, and her wootle was bright pink. The mom had asked, "How do you like your new little sister?"

Liam responded, "I like her, but I don't like when her pussy gets red." He started pulling me toward our car.

The mom looked up at me, shocked.

I just shrugged and said, " 'Vagina' is so clinical." Was it wrong? We say the word "puss" the way people say "pee-pee" instead of "penis."

Liam and I were halfway to the car, but I glanced back and saw that the look of shock hadn't faded. I ran back to her. "Just to clarify: She had a diaper rash but we used some Triple Paste. Totally under control now."

Now Dean and I sat with the kids on our bed in Malibu, preparing to break the news about number four. Dean took the lead: "You know when you open a letter and there's good news? Well, we have some good news."

Letters? What was he talking about? This wasn't a Publishers Clearing House sweepstakes! We were having a baby. The more he went on about letters, the more baffled Liam and Stella looked. Finally I blurted it out point-blank: "We're going to have another baby. A baby. Like Hattie."

Liam said, "Why do you keep having babies?" From his mouth to God's ears.

I said, "We love children. We love you guys. We want to give you brothers and sisters. You're okay, though? Okay that we're having another?"

Liam said, "Yeah, but when you're done with this one, can we have pillow fights again?"

Maybe Liam was onto something. I'd lose my baby weight doing postpartum pillow fights. It'd be the new mommy craze.

BACK ON *CRAFT Wars*, not everything was going perfectly. If I learned anything from *Tori & Dean* it was that I am in some ways my father's daughter, at least when it comes to looking at a show from the viewer's standpoint. I don't live in a Hollywood tower. I'm constantly talking to people through Twitter, my blog, book signings, even being out at the mall. I connect with viewers on a daily basis and feel like I have a clear sense of and instinct for what people want to see. On *Tori & Dean*, World of Wonder had given me a lot of freedom because they trusted me.

I thought *Craft Wars* was an excellent idea, but I didn't agree with the execution. The set looked the same as the producers' other show, *Cupcake Wars*. The name was practically the same. The judges sat in the same position. There were rows of crafting supplies like shears, glitter, ribbons, and fabric rolls on the wall where there had been cupcakes. The structure of the show was the same—the contestants worked at stations, participating in timed competitions on a stage. The cameras never recorded their personal interactions. They never followed them out into the real world or home. What worked for cupcakes didn't completely work for crafting. I wasn't sure about the contestants they'd picked or the ideas for the challenges. For instance, every challenge had a similar structure. We're making birdhouses . . . but we're going to do it using items found in a junk drawer. We're going to make jewelry . . . out of a boom box. We're going to make patio furniture . . . out of pool toys. As a viewer there was some intrigue—ooh, how are they going to pull this off? But for crafters, there should be a takeaway. It should give them ideas for things they could actually make and have in their living rooms. I wanted it to be aspirational.

In the producers' defense, when they were pre-

prepping I was out of town making *The Mistle-Tones*. By the time I arrived with all my brilliant ideas (that's a bit of self-aggrandizing, people), the show was already prepped.

I had made it clear from the beginning that I was not the person to be the onstage host reading off a teleprompter. Being that impersonal voice telling you the rules of the game isn't my strong suit. What I'm good at is talking to people and bantering. If it were *Project Runway*, I'd be more the Tim Gunn than the Heidi Klum. They said that they wanted me, with all my offbeat personality, and we agreed that I would pop in and offer ideas as the contestants worked. But in the edit room they cut whatever jokes I made and left only technical comments like "Are you sure that's the best glue to use?"

My fantasy was that *Craft Wars* would open the door for me to keep working with TLC, and maybe to grow my audience so that one day I would merit my own show. In the end, *Craft Wars* didn't end up being the show I hoped it would be. And, not surprisingly, it didn't get the viewers, it got canceled, and TLC lost interest in me. I'm only at four kids. Apparently you need nineteen to get a multiseason show with them.

To the Manor Born

In April, in the middle of filming *Craft Wars*, I went to New York to promote *celebraTORI*, my party-planning book. I was gone for two days, during which Dean moved us from Malibu to our elegant new rental in Westlake Village. I never said good-bye to Malibu. We'd lasted at that little house for less than six months, one of which was spent in Utah.

After selling our Encino house at a loss, we were hoping to make a bit of the money back on Malibu. We'd sunk a lot of money into it. There were all new appliances. And those gorgeous vintage wood floors I thought were my dream. Properties in Point Dume are hot properties. (Remember? That desirable school district?) That's why we'd moved so fast to buy the house. But our house took a few months to sell, and when it did, it was for two hundred thousand dollars *less* than we had paid. You hear about those people who flip houses to make money? We were the opposite: flippers who lost major sums of money on every transaction. My restlessness would be our financial ruin.

Our Westlake Village house was in a gated community. I loved the privacy. For the first time since I'd moved out of my first apartment in a high-rise apartment building on Wilshire Boulevard, there were no paparazzi parked on the street outside my house. The house was spacious and grand. I loved that it was on a single floor. That was great for the kids. I loved that there was a big eat-in kitchen attached to a den that opened out to the pool. It was the center of the house and when the kids were playing or eating we could all be right there together. I loved that it was near a lake and that it had views of the lake. There was a mini movie theater, and I fantasized about having family movie nights with freshly made popcorn. (I even ordered a popcorn machine, but we never used it. We literally watched one episode of *SpongeBob* and *The Mistle-Tones*. After that we never got the projector to work again.) I loved a lot about the house, but I hated the grandness of it, just as I'd hated the grandness of our Encino house. There were columns throughout the house, a huge chandelier, leaded glass windows, and cold stone floors mixed in with the nice hardwood. And it was way too big. Nine thousand square feet. Crazy! After Malibu, I'd gone to the opposite extreme. Our family was spread out again.

We couldn't afford to buy a house. Yet now we were living a lie in a grand house. Dean and I are usually good at balancing each other. But when I get excited, Dean gets excited. With this house I'd tried so hard to be careful. We came to look at it three times. It worked for us. But it was far away from everyone we knew and everything we did. Dean and I had to face the enormity of the mistakes we'd made. We never should have left Encino. We'd paid off that house. We'd had money in the bank.

In one of these hard conversations I said, "Well, it was part of our journey."

Dean said, "Home is not about the house. It's about the family."

I said, "I don't know if I've learned that." If we'd sold Malibu at a profit and had the money to buy another house, I'm pretty sure I would have made another rash decision. Who moves to Westlake Village? It was so fucking random. But here we were.

Liam and Stella started a new school. Liam was in kindergarten and Stella was in preschool. On Parents' Day, a mom came up to me and said, "We live behind the gates too." People in the community knew that we were renting, but most probably assumed we could afford to buy if we decided we wanted to.

I said, "Oh, that's great. We don't know anyone yet."

She said, "Have you joined the country club? It's a great way to meet neighbors." Our gated community had two clubs, the country club and the lake club. I didn't really know the difference, but I'd assumed that both were too expensive and I said so.

She said, "The least expensive membership is if you join the Lake Club just for tennis. You can play tennis, use the facilities, and go to the restaurant—you just can't use the golf course."

I said, "Oh! That sounds good!" It would be great to have a restaurant we could walk to without leaving the gates.

She said, "It's not bad at all. It's like forty thousand dollars a year."

Holy shit. Well, that was never gonna happen. I didn't want to sound lame, so I said, "Oh yeah, that's pretty good." Then, because now I was really curious, I asked if she knew how much it was with the golf.

She turned to her husband to ask. He smiled and said, "They just reduced the cost from two hundred to one hundred." One hundred thousand dollars to join the golf club. Good thing I can't stand golf.

The saddest and most ironic thing about our move to

Westlake Village was that it was the demise of our farm. The whole reason we'd left Encino was to indulge my fantasy of having a place to raise the animals. But the contract for the homeowners' association explicitly said, "No livestock." We'd moved from a farm with no house to a house with no farm.

It said no livestock, but I was hoping to bend the rules. We'd made an anonymous call to the homeowners' association asking about pigs. They said that a couple owners had them and that they "turned the other way when pigs were involved." Hank, it seemed, had a free pass. We didn't ask about the chickens and the goats. I didn't want to alert the authorities. But we knew from the start that our rooster, Jackson, had to go. He was really loud, what with all the cockadoodledooing at the crack of dawn.

Aw, Jackson. He wasn't quite as friendly as my chicken Coco, but he was cute and fluffy and pretty domesticated. We'd raised him from a baby. He knew his name and would follow me around. I wanted to find a good home for him, but I had no idea where to begin. Who was dying for a rooster?

When we moved from Malibu we left Jackson there in his coop. Someone went to feed him every day. Meanwhile I asked everyone on the planet if they wanted a rooster. Then I had a stroke of genius. I remembered that my agent Gueran represented Patrick Dempsey. Gueran had once told me that I would love Patrick's wife, Jill—because she loved farm animals as much as I did.

I e-mailed Gueran: "I know this is a long shot. This is Jackson. Do you think the Dempseys would want him?" I attached a picture.

Literally five minutes later I got an e-mail back from Gueran. "Bingo!" Jill had shown the picture of Jackson to her kids, and they loved him and wanted to take him. She told Gueran to give me her contact info.

The Dempseys decided to build Jackson his own coop. In the meantime, I tried to justify the move to myself. He'd be okay. He was upgrading celebrities. From Mc-Dermott to McDreamy.

Before I knew it, the Dempseys had agreed to take the two goats, too. My farm was being pulled out from under me. They had a huge space for them. The farm I dreamed of. See—it could be done! That's the difference between starring on a network drama versus a cable reality show. But one thing I actually learned from my brief Malibu experience was that having the animals outside, with plenty of room to roam about, wasn't my ideal either. I kind of liked it best when we lived in Encino and they were all bumbling around the kitchen with us. The goat chewed the corner of Liam's "all about me" board. Every time anyone opened the fridge, Hank would burrow his head in and grab the leftover yellowtail scallion rolls. They felt like part of the family.

Months later, while I was in the hospital, Dean dropped Hank off at the Dempseys' too. When he told me, he said, "I did it for him. It wasn't fair for him to live here." I hate to admit it, but I was kind of relieved to see Hank go. He wasn't the pig of my dreams. All he cared about was food. If you didn't have food he wasn't interested. In the yard he'd charge us to see if we had food. I was scared of my own pig.

Westlake Village was an answer, but in my heart of hearts I knew from the start that it wasn't the end of my wanderlust. It was a stopgap.

Complications

Craft Wars was filming in downtown L.A., over an hour away from our new place. My call time was six in the morning, so we left my house at five. We frequently worked until nine P.M., and I spent most of the day on my feet, in high heels, pregnant. Sometimes, after a particularly long or grueling day, the production company would put me up in the Ritz-Carlton downtown so I wouldn't have to drive all the way back home just to turn around and head straight back. (NB: It wasn't a fancy Ritz—just one of those business-y ones that might as well be a Marriott. There might have been a pillow menu, but that was the only Ritz of it.) Halfway through, when

they found out I was pregnant, they gave me a chair to sit
down in between takes.

One night, at the end of April, I stayed at the Ritz after
a super-long day. My makeup artist, Brandy, kept me
company. The next morning, I woke up, went to the bathroom, and sat down to pee. It was like a horror movie. The
toilet filled with blood. I had the same terror response as
last time: my heart dropped into my toes, and my fingers
went numb. I yelled for Brandy: "I'm bleeding!"

Ever since the incident on the massage table at eight
weeks pregnant, everything had been fine. Now I asked
Brandy, "Do you think I'm having a miscarriage? Is the
baby going to be okay?" Brandy is always very nurturing and maternal, but all she could say was, "It's a lot of
blood. I honestly don't know."

I took a photo of the blood and sent it to Dr. J. Then
I got into bed and put a pillow under my feet. While I
waited to hear from him, I kept my hand on my wootle,
as if I could stop the blood or hold in the baby.

There were two obligations I had that day. The first was
a photo shoot for *Craft Wars*. Then there were these little
webisodes called *What Would Tori Do?* that we were filming
to promote the show. Whatever craft the contestants were
racing to do on the show, I would make my version. Both
commitments had crews on hand—with both combined,
nearly fifty people were probably standing by. I had to

find out right away if I could work today or whether they should call it an insurance day, which meant, with a doctor's excuse, everything would be canceled and covered by the production's insurance company.

When Dr. J called back, he was about to go into surgery. He said, "A bleed is a bleed, it doesn't make a difference if you lie down or go to work today."

I said, "Okay, but I just want to be clear. It's a fifteen-hour day, and I'll spend most of it standing in high heels." He said that if I felt more comfortable I could meet with a doctor in his office, Dr. Mandel, before I did.

I decided to go ahead with the photo shoot that morning. I scheduled an appointment with Dr. Mandel for afterward and told the *Craft Wars* people that if the doctor said it was okay, I'd be back to film the webisode afterward.

For the photo shoot I wore a turquoise tulle prom dress with a voluminous skirt. My necklace was a crafty confection of colored pencils. We took a bunch of shots of me in various hammy poses: holding a bedazzled glue gun as if I were in a Western; throwing confetti up in the air. I plastered a showman smile on my face, all the while thinking, *Oh my God, am I having a miscarriage?* As soon as we were done, I got in the car and went straight to the doctor.

Dean met me at the doctor's office. Dr. Mandel diagnosed me on the spot with placenta previa, which explained the bleeding. My placenta had formed over my cervix. Trust me, it's not ideal. Then he told me that I wasn't going back to work—he wanted me on bed rest for the next four days. The tear in the placenta would heal itself if I stayed off my feet.

I didn't know exactly what bed rest was, but it sounded nice. Dr. Mandel explained that he wanted me to spend most of the next few days lying down. I could move from the bed to the couch and turn on the TV, but I should stay flat on my back while I watched. Frankly, it was a relief. I'd gone from doing a very physical movie straight to *Craft Wars*. I'd done an HSN segment in the middle of *Craft Wars*, then gone to New York to promote my party-planning book, then back to *Craft Wars*. All while pregnant. My body was done. But I would never have canceled work. It was nice to have a doctor tell me that I had no choice.

Dropping the webisodes wasn't a disaster, but I still had to shoot the final episode of *Craft Wars* the next day. I hoped we could do it the next week, but the show came back to me saying that they had all the contestants, the judges, and the sets, and the show had to wrap on time in order to make room for another show that was taping in the same space. They ended up taping the final episode with one of the on-set experts, a guy named Steve. I never went back—I never even got to say good-bye to the crew.

I'd left my unfinished Mod Podge doily tray on set. I'm sure it's gathering dust in some TLC prop room.

When the show aired, nobody knew about my illness. The viewers saw me hosting every week, and then the final week I just wasn't there. There was no explanation or fanfare for the finale. They aired it back-to-back with another episode. It was a sad whimper of an ending.

THAT WEEKEND BROOKE Burke filled in for me at a My Little Pony kids' event. She tweeted, "hi @torianddean I hope you feel better. In the spirit of friendship, I was happy to b there 4 u today & we all missed you!"

Brooke and I both have busy mommy lives and usually catch up with each other via personal e-mail. When we moved to Malibu, where her family lived, we thought we'd have playdates but it never happened. It was weird to me that she had expressed her sympathy through Twitter. She couldn't possibly have known what I was really going through. Or maybe people are starting to think that Twitter is a normal way to reach out. It just made me kind of sad.

I was supposed to take it easy at home all weekend, but on Sunday Dean was out working all day. I was home with the housekeeper and the three kids. All day I was picking up Hattie, moving her from the bouncy chair, to the high chair, to the floor. To top it off, I was determined to be the first person to take Hattie swimming in the pool. I shouldn't have done it. It was too much. By that night I had cramps and a little bleeding, and on Monday morning I had a big bleed, my third. I went to the hospital, Cedars. The high-risk doctor who saw me there thought that I might have placenta accreta, an even more serious complication. They decided to keep an eye on me for a week.

While I was at Cedars under observation, an amazing thing happened. One of my best friends, Amy, had her baby. I was already at the hospital waiting for her! Our mutual doctor, Dr. J, wheeled me to Amy's room, where she was in labor.

Amy's family is big and very close, and they were all there for the big event: her parents, her two brothers, her sister-in-law, her teenage niece, her in-laws, and another friend. Mehran and I squeezed into her room. When Amy's family saw me in my wheelchair, everyone gasped.

Amy said, "She's fine. Don't ask a million questions." That was Amy, managing people even while in labor.

Everyone (except me) sat on the floor with pillows and blankets, telling stories and taking turns napping. A nurse brought in a box of Popsicles. We didn't sing "Kumbaya," but the idea came up. Part of me was like, *Oh my God, I would never want this.* But at the same time I thought,

Wow, it's so nice that they all want to be here. In the early-morning hours we were all punch-drunk, trying to stay awake. Amy's father was telling bad jokes, trying to keep spirits up, and someone was busting out old vacation photos. At some point I said, "Hey, guys. Want to see a funny shit my son took?" I passed around my phone, on which I had a picture of said shit. Liam had pooped a cock and balls. Nobody was shocked or horrified. What a great family. I sat there, in my wheelchair, all night long. When Amy was ready to push, everyone filed into the waiting room and I went back to my room.

A COUPLE HOURS later Amy's sister-in-law came into my room looking worried.

"Amy's not in her delivery room anymore. We went to check on her, but she's just gone. We don't know where she is." The family was freaking out.

I figured she'd been taken away for a Cesarean. As a C-section veteran, I asked them to wheel me down the hall to reassure her family. I didn't want the people in the waiting area to see me, so we were all huddled at the end of a long hallway. Some of Amy's family members were crying. I was telling them that C-sections are actually really safe. Then we looked up. Dr. J, in his scrubs, was coming down the hall. It was like a slo-mo scene from

Grey's Anatomy. He gave us a double thumbs-up, and everyone started cheering and hugging.

I got to go into the recovery room to visit with Amy and meet the baby for the first time. Her name was Anika. And I didn't have to drive all the way from Westlake Village to see her. It was perfect timing.

The next night, around three in the morning, I startled awake. Someone was standing next to me. It was Amy, in her robe, crying.

"Something's happened," she said. "Anika had a seizure."

I sat straight up.

"She was in the nursery. I didn't see it," she said. Anika recovered, but she would have to stay in the hospital for weeks.

They released me on a Monday. Amy was staying for one more day, so on my way out a cute and fabulous male nurse, Adam, wheeled me to her room. Amy's whole family was in the room, and I said good-bye to all of them.

Adam wheeled me to the parking lot, where Dean was waiting with the car. As we pulled away, I started unexpectedly weeping. I'd had no idea how sad I would be to leave Amy's family. For the three days they'd been around the hospital, I felt like they were my family too. They'd taken turns coming to my room, bringing me food. Even Amy's mother-in-law, whom I didn't know well, would come and sit with me for an hour at a time. She cared about me. She wanted to keep me occupied. I loved her family for that. And now it was ending. I cried all the way home.

Later, I told Amy how sad I'd been. "I really have to re-connect with your family. When Liam and Stella were ba-bies we used to spend Christmases together. I miss them. I was sad to leave them."

Amy said, "You can have them! You can see them whenever you want. I don't know why you'd want to, but you can."

I WAS FINE for that week in the hospital, but the fact was that I was having more and more bleeds. This time, Cedars only agreed to release me on the condition that I move ten to fifteen minutes from the hospital. Dr. Silverman, the high-risk doctor who was overseeing my case, kept refer-ring to our house in Westlake Village as Woodland Hills. He'd say, "You really can't live as far away as Woodland Hills." Woodland Hills, which he saw as impossibly far, was half an hour closer than our house.

I was thinking, *Fuck, I wish I lived that close.*

They said I had to be near the hospital for the rest of the pregnancy. As soon as we got home I started trolling the web, looking for a temporary place to live. We were moving . . . again. My mother agreed to help us out with the rent, but we needn't have bothered. I would be back in the hospital in less than a week.

Dean and Liam were having a boys' night, sleeping together in Liam's room, and Stella and I were having a girls' night in the master bedroom. This was normal for us—we have very fluid sleeping arrangements. The kids are always in and out of our bedroom.

Stella was already asleep, but I stayed up late that night. The next day, May 7, was Dean's and my sixth anniversary. I wanted to write a love poem for Dean, and I decided to tackle it at midnight. My first draft was in the notes section of my iPhone—I'd have to write it out the next morning—and I was really going for it, rhyming and everything.

The next morning I woke at six A.M. in a pool of blood. When I stood up blood ran down my legs. I'd never seen so much blood. It was like a massacre had occurred. I got myself to the toilet, hoping it would stop, but it didn't. I thought I was going to bleed to death. Dean was all the way at the other end of the house. There was no way he'd hear me if I called. I needed to wake up Stella for help. I took a moment to think about this. Stella was only almost four. I didn't want her to see me in this condition—and there was blood all over the bathroom—but what else could I do? I didn't feel like I had a choice.

"Stella!" I called out. "Stella!"

"Yes, Mommy?" I heard. She came to the doorway, rubbing sleep out of her eyes.

There was a chance this wouldn't work. Children are so stoned sometimes. Stella could get the munchies or decide to do a jigsaw puzzle en route to Liam's room. On the other hand, I didn't want to terrify her. "Go get Daddy and tell him I'm bleeding," I said. I tried to convey urgency, but a confident, maternal urgency, if there is such a thing.

My girl did her job. When Dean came in and saw the bloody scene, he was calm as always.

"Should I take a picture for Dr. J?" I said.

"No," he said. "We're going to head to the hospital." He helped clean me up and got me dressed. By the time we got in the car, the bleeding seemed to have stopped. We called Dr. J, who said that if it started again we would have to get off the freeway and go to the closest hospital, but we made it to Cedars.

Then, after I'd been in my room for less than an hour, I started bleeding again. Dr. J was still en route, so a resident was taking care of me. He told the nurses to prep the operating room for me. If the bleeding didn't stop they would remove the fetus and the placenta so I didn't lose too much blood and die. I was beside myself with fear and sadness.

But when Dr. J arrived, he checked the pad and said that we weren't close to that point yet. He said, "Sometimes I think with celebrities the residents panic more." Now Dr. J took the time to explain all the steps we would take to stop the bleeding without ending the pregnancy. But he said, "I'm not going to put your life in danger. The baby is not viable at this point. I'm going to save you over your baby."

Then he said, "You know you're not leaving here, right? You're here for a good long while."

And that was how Dean and I celebrated our sixth anniversary. In the hospital. I was five months pregnant, and I would spend the next two and a half months in the hospital.

The Glamorous Life

Bed rest, which had seemed so relaxing when I first heard about it, took on a whole new meaning. I wasn't allowed out of bed. I lay flat on my back. At first I wasn't allowed to walk to the bathroom or to take a shower. I peed in a portable potty that stood next to my bed (but I insisted on doing my number twos in the bathroom—I tried to preserve a shred of dignity. No way was I crapping in a commode). They drew blood every other day so that there was always fresh blood on hand in case I needed a transfusion.

A rotation of nurses came in to take my vitals, check my baby monitor, and clean my commode. I'd only been there a couple nights when one of my night nurses said, "Do you like this room?"

"I don't know anything different," I said.

She said, "Well, a couple of the rooms across the way are better. The configuration gives you a little more space, and there's a nicer view. It seems like the woman in one of them went home tonight. Want me to see if that room is available?"

I wasn't sure. Even moving across the hall seemed dangerous for the baby. But this night nurse was on the case. She took pictures of the room with her phone and brought them back to me. It did look nicer! (In that dubious, incremental way that one hospital room can have a leg up on another.)

At two A.M. the night nurse came back into my room. I was sitting on the commode when she entered—this quickly became fairly routine, that I'd be sitting there when the nurses came in. I was already used to peeing in front of Mehran and showing my poops to Dean. It wasn't a huge transition. Anyway, the nurse told me the new room she'd scouted for me was available, and I could move right now. When I looked hesitant, she added, "It's a good-luck room. Lots of A-list people have stayed in it, like Julia Roberts."

"Julia Roberts stayed there?" I said.

"I can't really say," she said.

I knew Julia Roberts's babies had turned out just fine. Maybe it *was* a good-luck room. Besides, it would be yet another thing Julia Roberts and I had in common. We both thought the paparazzi should back off . . . and one day, I hoped, we both would have babies who had gestated in room one.

So what if it was the middle of the night? Day and night have less meaning in a hospital. My bed was on wheels, so the nurse pushed me straight into the other room. I rolled into the new bed, and that was it. Upgrade complete. It was the hospital version of my compulsive house-hunting and moving.

THE NURSES KNEW that I was in the hospital for the long haul, and soon they started asking when I was going to start decorating. They told me that a lot of long-term moms with high-risk pregnancies decorated to make the hospital feel more like home. We moms-to-be could do anything that wasn't permanent. The nurses had seen our show and read my blog and knew that I loved decorating, so they said, "We can't wait to see what you're going to do!" They told me about one mom who had turned her room into a chic New York apartment, complete with an area rug, a standing lamp, curtains, lights, and wall art. The gauntlet was thrown. If I was going to be holed up here for the rest of my pregnancy, I needed something to focus on. I decided to go for it.

In my decorating life I had gone from the feminine pastels of shabby chic, to a white leather and grass-green modern palette (it was a moment), to Regency black lacquer and peacocks. I grew up in a room my mother had decorated in plum florals. I'd never had the chance to live in a bright pink girly room. Now was my opportunity. I wanted the room to be bright and happy and poppy and girly. Time to call in the gays! Much as I loved him, I couldn't work with James on this. I knew James—who was my partner in crime for the wedding shows—would want the room to have leather club chairs and old rugs from England. What I wanted—James would kill himself first. But Bill and Scout have great taste, and they like midcentury modern with pops of color. I enlisted them to help.

Their most amazing find was temporary wallpaper that basically peels on like contact paper. It was turquoise with a gold pattern on it—kind of midcentury meets Regency. Dean agreed to hang it, and we put it on the wall facing my bed. It was a very bold color and pattern. I worried that I'd get sick of it. But every morning when I woke up, that paper made me happy. I'd look at it and smile.

We replaced the hospital curtain that surrounded my

bed and put up a shower curtain I'd found that looked sort of like a modern white doily. There was a hot-pink metal table, a white love seat, and framed photos of the kids on the wall. On the floor was a rag rug made of turquoise, pink, and canary yellow. There were brocade pillows and gold accents. By the time Bill and Scout executed my vision, my room looked girly dorm room meets chic Parisian apartment. James walked in and grimaced.

"I know you hate it. You hate the color. I know. I just wanted something different. This is what I wanted. Fun. Happy. Girly."

James said, "No, it's great," but I knew he was vomiting on the inside.

DEAN CAME ALMOST every day and stayed with me for hours. He slept over every Tuesday night—that was our "date night," and boy, was I a hot date. After all, I spent all my time horizontal.

Stella, Liam, and Hattie only came to visit once or twice a week. They were still in school in the deep Valley, with karate and ballet after school. I didn't want to disrupt their lives. I never got a sense that they missed me too much. All I had was time to miss them all day long, but they were so young. Moments happen, then are forgotten. They were always happy to see me—or at least the cupcakes I'd been given—but as soon as they left, they were on to the next fun thing.

For the most part I didn't want any visitors beyond my immediate family. Usually I want to entertain my friends, but now I was lying there, too scared to move. A monitor showed that whenever I had visitors, like Mehran and my mother, my contractions increased, putting the baby at further risk. When the doctors saw me having contractions, they would tell my guests that I had to rest. I didn't mind when they left—the truth was I barely had the energy to talk.

Eventually I settled into a routine. Every day for breakfast I'd order bacon, a bagel, and cream cheese. If I was feeling frisky, I'd get scrambled eggs to go on the bagel. Some weeks I switched to yogurt parfait. Once I shocked the hell out of Joyce in Food and Nutrition when I spontaneously opted for a croissant with butter and jelly. Breakfast came at eight, but as the nurses got to know me, they realized I liked to sleep in and they'd bring my breakfast last, at eight thirty.

Dr. J checked on me every day. It was often the bright spot of my day. We'd talk about his love life, and he'd eat all of my crispy bacon and bring me fun treats like Sour Patch Kids.

When I didn't have visitors, I watched a lot of TV.

Every night for dinner I'd order a fully loaded baked

potato and corn with butter and salt on the side. Some-times, to mix it up, I'd get the apple pie for my dessert instead of my standard berry pie. Dinner arrived at seven, and afterward I'd do a little web surfing, either picking out vintage teacups on Etsy for Stella's fourth birthday party, blogging for my website, shopping on Gilt, or post-ing images on Instagram. I even changed the default ship-ping address for my online purchases to Cedars-Sinai, care of the Maternal-Fetal Care Unit. Nobody knew I was in the hospital, but if you look at my Instagram post-ings from that time, all the photos are super-close-up im-ages of my hospital dinners, the nail art I did on myself during the long hours in my hospital bed, cupcakes or flowers that people brought me, and lots of pictures of doughnuts. You can see my hospital tray and bits of the room in the background. There's a shot of me wearing a rhinestone headpiece that I made, below which I wrote "2 much to wear to the grocery store?" The truth was that at that point a trip to the grocery store would have been super exciting. It's hard for a body to know when and how much to sleep when it spends all day in bed, so I often fell asleep sitting straight up with my glasses on and my hands suspended above the laptop keyboard in the middle of buying yet another glamorous maxi dress on Gilt. They may take my mobility, but they'll never take my caftans. (*Braveheart*, anyone?)

There were breaks from the routine. One night a nurse came in, took one look at me, and said, "I'm going to wash your hair for you." She was right. I needed it. I had limited shower privileges, so I had tried using dry shampoo. My hair came out terribly. So now the nurse used a bowl to wash my hair in the hospital bed. Then she brought in another nurse and one of them used a blow dryer while the other flat-ironed the part that was already dry. While they worked, we watched Kardashian reruns, gossiped about Kim Kardashian's rumored ass implants, and giggled. Then one of the nurses pointed to an unopened box that had arrived from Gilt days earlier.

She said, "What is that? It's been there forever."

I said, "I did a little shopping, but I can't get up to open it."

She said, "Well, let's open it right now."

The nurses took out about ten maxi dresses and caftans. The two of them held them up and sashayed across my room. This was midnight on a Sunday night. It was a total slumber party. I wanted to suggest playing "light as a feather, stiff as a board," but I didn't want the fetus to get a complex.

EVERY TUESDAY AT noon Patti, my Reiki therapist/practitioner, came to see me. I looked forward to our sessions, not just because they were a break in the monotony of the hospital, but because Patti changed the way I saw myself and my situation. Reiki is a kind of alternative healing practice. Patti would put on calming music and I would close my eyes. She would hover her hands above me. It was like a massage, but with no actual contact. An energy massage. Afterward, Patti would tell me things like, "The baby wants avocados."

Whenever Patti thought the baby wanted a certain food, I would call right down to the hospital chef, Darrell. For my birthday, my mother had generously upgraded me to the "special menu" at the hospital. This meant that instead of the regular hospital fare, I got a slightly better menu. Every day I was supposed to call down to put in my order.

Darrell was the voice at the other end of the line. He and I would never meet, but we had a very special phone-kitchen relationship. If I ran late placing my order, Darrell would call and say, "It's Darrell. It's seven thirty and I haven't heard from you. What can I make you?"

I'd say, "I can't decide on anything right now."

He'd say, "Let's go off-menu. What do you like, Chinese food? Chicken? Steak? Do you want fried rice with steak in it?"

"That sounds amazing!" I'd say.

He'd ask what vegetables I wanted mixed in the stir-fry. Whenever the kitchen staff brought up my food they'd say, "Darrell says hi." It made everything a little more personal.

Maybe it was the sensory deprivation of the hospital bed, but Darrell sounded cool. I always wondered what he looked like. And I wondered if he knew who I was or just bonded with me because of our phone rapport.

Another time Darrell had made something special for me. The kitchen staff seemed to be all female, but this time a guy brought it up. He was cute, Asian, maybe in his thirties. I was on the phone when he came in. He put the tray down and said, "Have a great day." I thought I recognized the voice. Was it Darrell? I couldn't interrupt the call to find out, and so I never got to meet my phone friend face-to-face.

Anyway, one Tuesday Patti came in and started working. She told me that the placenta previa had happened as a wake-up call for me. I go, go, go and don't know my own limits. The baby wanted me to focus on the pregnancy. He wanted my complete attention. This was why I was on bed rest. So I could focus on him. Also, he wanted a steak.

Again, we hadn't let Dr. J tell us the baby's gender, but Dean and I and everyone else was again convinced that we were having a boy. Patti reminded me that she'd felt baby male energy radiating from me before Hattie was even conceived. She said that the baby in my womb was supposed to have been Hattie's twin but he missed the portal. That was why he slipped in at the first opportunity, right behind Hattie.

As Patti spoke I was visualizing the baby and Hattie, and his little soul's determination to live and be close to his sister. Images of Hattie flashed through my mind, and I envisioned sharing them with the baby. I know it sounds weird, but I felt as though he liked seeing her. The three of us were connected.

Patti and I worked through some of my biggest fears. That I would lose the baby. That the kids would lose their mother. That Hattie was so young, she would forget she'd ever had a mother. Patti told me that worry does nothing but manifest things.

"You have to tell yourself that the baby is safe because it's in you. All of this"—she swept her arm out, indicating the hospital, the room, and me in the bed—"through all of this, the baby has succeeded in getting your attention. Have faith. That's all you can do at this point. It's not about God or religion. When I say 'have faith,' I mean that you have to believe in yourself."

It was hard. I thought about a visit I'd had with Stella and Hattie. It was a sweet, all-girls afternoon during which Stella sat on a tuft and, using a box as a makeshift table, painted a little birdhouse. But when it was time for them to head home with their nanny, Paola, Stella didn't want to go. Crying hysterically, she said she wanted to stay and sleep with Mama. I felt completely helpless. It had taken Dean getting on the phone with her and promising that he'd bring her back the next day to calm her down. My hospitalization was definitely the hardest challenge Stella had faced so far in her short life. Taking Patti's advice meant rising above my own feelings of helplessness to help Stella see that this was a journey for all of us, and that we would come through it together.

After Patti left, the Shirelles song "Will You Still Love Me Tomorrow" came into my head. "Tonight you're mine completely / You give your love so sweetly." Alone in my hospital room, I sang that song to my unborn child and felt a little bit of peace.

ONE WEEKEND THE whole family stayed across the street at the Sofitel Hotel. When they came to see me on Saturday, Liam and Stella gave me big warm hugs. Liam immediately focused on ravaging the Skittles and Sour Patch Kids that Bill and Scout had brought me. But Stella climbed up on the bed, looked me over closely, and then asked, "Mama, are you ever coming home from the hospital?"

It broke my heart. Wasn't I asking myself the same question? But I buried my feelings, put on a bright smile, and said, "Of course, mama. The doctors just want me to stay at the hospital for a little while to keep me and the baby safe." Stella seemed satisfied with that—I wished I were so easily comforted.

We snuck Liam and Stella into my room so they could spend the night and wake up with me the next day. Only one cot fit in the room, so Dean stayed with Hattie and Patsy in the hotel right across the street. The kids slept on the cot next to me. As usual, I woke up several times in the middle of the night to the soft light of the medical monitors and beeps from rooms nearby. It didn't feel as lonely with my babies lying close to me, the sound of their soft breath filling the room with life. A mother's job is to create, love, and nurture. I felt helpless, but I was doing all I could for my growing baby. Nurturing it by staying in the hospital. Keeping it safe. In that moment my hospital room felt as close to home as it could get.

The next morning Stella gave me a sunflower she had painted. It went straight up on the wall. Liam had made me a recipe-card holder in school. Clipped to it was a recipe. His teachers had written it out for him. It was his favorite thing to cook: mashed potatoes. In the card he wrote, "I love when you make me breakfast and going shopping with you."

It was a momentous day because for the first time Dr. J allowed me to be wheeled out to the plaza level to get some fresh air. The air and sun on my face felt good. I sat in my wheelchair smiling and watched Liam and Stella chase each other all around, screaming and laughing. Dean held Hattie, who smiled a big gummy smile and squealed every time they zoomed past her. This was my family, but at the same time as I felt like the center of it, I also felt disconnected. It was strange to be watching from the sidelines. I'm usually in there, playing chase, then panting for twenty minutes and cursing myself for not working out in four years.

I thought about my dad. When I was growing up, he was always the life of the party, holding court, telling stories. But in the last few years of his life, after he had throat cancer, he was different. He was in remission, but he seemed much older. His zest for life was gone. As my brother Randy, our friends, and I laughed and told stories, he just sat quietly in the corner chair or his bed, kind of smiling, kind of zoned out. At the time I was hurt that he seemed distracted or disinterested, but now I got it. When you really can't participate it's hard to be present. Your body gets in the way of what your mind and heart want.

After a sunny half hour out in the real world, we came back inside. As we approached the elevator, I saw sign with an arrow pointing left. It said "Gift Shop." Shopping? I'd take any form of a retail-therapy fix.

When we entered the gift shop I gasped in glee, shouting, "It's huge!"

Dean said, "It's not that big." Buzzkill.

I had Dean wheel me all over that shop, and I was especially taken with a pair of coral Isotoner slippers. Funny how when almost everything is stripped away, the smallest things become more colorful and exciting.

When they announced the gift shop was closing, I settled on a copy of *Redbook* magazine, which featured easy summer entertaining tips that I would most certainly not have a chance to execute, and a pack of hair bands so I could practice my fish-tail braids in my new life of leisure.

We'd all been so happy for me to get outside, and yet I had an unexpected sense of relief when I came back to my room. The truth was that my brightly colored dorm room had become my world. I felt like the fetus inside me was safe there, and being out on the sunny plaza only reminded me that an outside world still existed, and I was missing out on it.

SEVERAL DAYS LATER, Dr. Silverman came by with the 3-D ultrasound machine. It had been two weeks since his last visit, and I was anxious to see if the baby was okay. I was always anxious to know if the baby was okay. Dr. Silverman ran the cold ultrasound wand over my belly and I heard the baby's quick little heartbeat. He was still there, strong and steady. Looking at the screen, Dr. Silverman gave a big smile. He said the placenta had moved into a slightly better position. I didn't understand everything he said, but this was very good news.

"You're no longer a ticking time bomb," he said.

"Well, what am I now?" I joked.

"I've upgraded you to a firecracker," he said. I loved that Dr. Silverman.

I was twenty-four weeks along. The baby was considered viable. He told me that he had considered giving me steroid injections at this point in the pregnancy to develop the baby's lungs in case there was an emergency and they had to deliver the baby. But I'd gone several weeks without a bleed. Now he was no longer as worried and wanted to hold off on the steroids. If things kept improving, at some point the danger would pass and I could go home. He wanted me to know about the possibility, but he didn't want to get my hopes up too far.

In that moment I grasped how serious my situation had been, and at the same time I felt optimism on the horizon. Before he'd come in to look at the ultrasound, I had told myself that no matter what he saw, I would remain positive. I would get myself and my baby through this. When Dr. Silverman left, I looked up and thanked God and my angels. I sat holding my belly and bawled my eyes out. I cried and cried, blissfully happy, but also scared to be too happy yet.

I was still crying when I called Dean to report on the doctor's visit. I knew he would be worried when he heard my shaky voice, so through my tears I blurted out, "I got good news!" As Patti had recommended, I had done all I could do. I had had faith. Faith in me, faith in my baby, faith in my family, and faith in the life I would continue to build with them. Now I was hearing words of encouragement. It felt like my positivity had paid off. Today was a milestone.

Reality Check

The next time Patti came for our weekly session, Dr. J and Amy were keeping me company when she arrived. As they left the room, Dr. J said to Patti, "Move that placenta!" He's a medical doctor, so he was a bit cynical about Patti's spiritual mumbo jumbo, but Patti was truly helping me take charge of my emotional state.

I told her the good news from Dr. Silverman but quickly added that I was scared to get too excited. Patti always sees things from an angle I can't anticipate. She said, "Don't think about wanting an outcome or not getting the outcome you want. Just be hopeful in the moment. Stay present and have hope." It was so simple, so clear and direct. By the time our session was over, I was brimming with hope.

Then I checked my e-mail. Sitting in my inbox was a message from my agent Ruthanne. It said, "I tried to call you but couldn't reach you. I hate to tell you by e-mail, but I want you to hear it from me: Oxygen called. They said the network is moving in a different direction and the show is canceled. I'm so sorry. Let's talk as soon as you're ready." I couldn't believe it. *Tori & Dean* was over? The show had been our life—literally—for six years.

I flashed back to another time when bad news had come to me electronically. I was in Toronto with Dean when I got the news that my sitcom, *So noTORIous*, had been unceremoniously canceled. This was the same sinking feeling. A feeling of loss and powerlessness. All that work with so many people I loved uniting to create a show I was proud of. Then some executives made a decision and it was over, just like that.

Adding insult to injury, after all these years working together, sharing my life and family with them on-screen, nobody from the network had even bothered to contact me personally.

For six years *Tori & Dean* had followed our lives. It was a reality show. Having it rejected felt like our lives—or the story of us—was being rejected. Before I called Ruthanne, or Dean, or anyone else to process this news, I put my phone down and rested my head back against the pillow, crying silently, thinking about the journey Dean and I had taken in the course of making the show.

AS MOST PEOPLE know, the lines of reality in reality TV get blurred. Our lives might be interesting enough for TV, but there is still no such thing as straight documentary, ever, in film or TV. They can't just turn on a camera, run it nonstop for hours on end, and then air the tape from start to finish. Everything has to be edited to have a structure. Everything needs to be given a narrative shape.

The very first season of the show had a really straightforward hook. Dean and I were going to open a bed-and-breakfast together, and I was pregnant with our first child. All of that was real, but it also meant we all knew in advance where the show was going. I was a fish out of water, a Beverly Hills girl trying to start a small business in the middle of nowhere.

After we'd proven ourselves in the first season and shown that we could draw an audience, they still wanted us to give them a sense of what might happen at the beginning of each season. This exercise always frustrated me. It was our lives! How could I predict what was going to happen by episode ten? The most I could do was give them general guidelines, like where I was with new businesses, how I was juggling family and career, the ups and downs in my relationship with Dean, and what milestones the kids were hitting. As far as I was concerned, it didn't matter what we plotted out on paper. Those plans were never what made the show work. It was the unexpected that happened along the way. Crazy things just seemed to happen to us.

Once, at a farmers' market, a fan approached me and started talking about *90210* as if it had actually happened. She asked how David (my on-screen boyfriend) was and whether Kelly (my fictional best friend) was still my roommate at our beach apartment. I loved it because it was a real, quirky encounter. Networks try so hard to put together "softly scripted" shows, but you couldn't script that kind of comedy if you tried. With our show it seemed to all fall into place. We encountered wonderfully eccentric characters, like Giselle, who worked on an ostrich farm. I loved her. Who could predict that Scout would fly off a bucking bronco at a dude ranch? Or that my dear and perfect toddler Liam would spontaneously curse (actually, that's shamefully more predictable than it should be—we left it in once but most of the time we edited it out). Anyway, I worried that if we planned too much, we'd strip the show of the spontaneity and raw truth that drew people to reality TV in the first place.

Once a season got going, there were all sorts of edits

we had to make along the way in order to tell a cohesive story. There were also some great moments that we had to edit out of *Tori & Dean*. One time Dean and I were in the kitchen having a heated parenting debate. Just as we asked Patsy which of us she thought was right, her phone started ringing. Patsy's ringtone was some disco groove. Everyone in the room—Dean, me, the cameramen, the producers—we all stopped what we were doing and danced to the ringing phone. Then it stopped and we immediately picked up the conversation where we'd left off.

Another day we were filming and suddenly we heard dogs barking and looked out our kitchen window to see the production assistant run past the window, arms flailing, screaming in real fear. Chasing him were all four of our dogs, on the attack. He hurled himself over a fence. He wasn't badly injured, but the dogs had ripped holes in his jeans in a not-fashionable way. It was a very scary, dramatic, and very *real* moment, but we couldn't include it as part of our story because he was part of the production crew, and even though we'd become friendly with him, he wasn't a "character" on the show.

We'd become close with all of our crew, especially Mario, the director of photography and lead camera guy. Mario knew when and how to be discreet. Once, in the first season, we had a barbecue at the inn. It was a family-friendly affair, with a bouncy house, a Slip 'n Slide, and a petting zoo. My friends Suzanne and Scout were in character costumes to entertain the kids. I'd just given birth to Liam, so I was wearing a maxi dress with Spanx underneath. They happened to be the kind of Spanx that have a pee hole. (I never found the pee hole practical. There's a reason girls' pants don't have flies.) Anyway, the bouncy house we rented had a built-in slide. Suzanne and I decided to go down it while Mario was at the base, filming. I threw myself onto the slide. As I went down, my dress flew up. My legs were spread, and, as Dean would put it, I blew a lip.

Poor Mario. He had to see that through his lens. As I stood up and pulled myself together, I said, "Mo, did you see that?"

He said, "Yeah, I'll rewind and delete." It was thanks to Mario that Oxygen never saw the dailies with me flashing my pussy. Maybe we should have left the snatch shot in. After all, their show *Bad Girls Club* is still on the air.

We also reenacted some moments, like when I took the pregnancy test with Mehran. Redoing scenes didn't bother me at all. It was the real drama of my real life; we just tweaked it a little so it made sense for the story line and was entertaining for the viewers.

It's hard for me to watch reality shows without the setup scenes jumping out at me. In *Keeping Up with the Kardashians*, there'll be a scene, early in an episode, that seems casual and incidental, like the one where Khloé and Kourtney are riding in an elevator, Khloé thinks something smells bad, and they blame it on a food delivery guy who is in the elevator with them. Later, Khloé tells Kourtney's boyfriend Scott that it was actually Kourtney's body odor that she smelled in the elevator. When I saw the elevator scene, I didn't know that the plot was going to revolve around Kourtney's BO, but I knew that scene was a setup. I could smell it a mile away—much farther than the reach of Kourtney's alleged BO. There are no random scenes in reality television.

WHAT HAPPENED AT the end of our fifth season was a perfect example of a time when I felt like the lines of reality got blurred. Dean and I had been fighting, and our relationship issues were central to the story line. As the season drew to a close, we talked about how it was going to end. I'm a sucker for a fairy-tale ending. I knew what the perfect ending would be. Renewing our vows.

Dean and I weren't really there yet. I knew we'd get there, but not in time for the end of the season. And it was about to be our fourth anniversary. In ordinary circumstances, even if I'd felt like Dean and I were back to normal, I would have waited until our fifth anniversary. I knew it was the right thing to do. But I wouldn't have done it right then if it weren't for the show, and that's the honest truth.

After the vow renewals came season six. Just as we'd shifted season five to show that Dean and I were having issues, we'd shifted season six to focus on my pregnancy with Hattie.

In the past few months, before I'd gone into the hospital for my fourth pregnancy, we'd been jumping through hoops trying to make the next season, season seven, happen. Moving to Malibu might have been a great setup for a change in life, but we'd already left Malibu behind. When I told the network that I'd be having a fourth baby, they all but said, "We've already done three babies."

They felt the same way about the kids' birthday parties. They thought our lives were too repetitive. Maybe I was too close to it, but I'd always thought that the core of what made our show work wasn't the parties or the projects or the pregnancies—it was all the little and big things that went wrong or right in the course of our lives. To me, nixing one of our kids' birthday parties as "overdone" was like telling the writers of *The Office* that the characters shouldn't keep going to the office every day.

For two months now we'd been in creative talks with the network trying to find ways to reinvent the show. We talked about making it more raw, home video–esque. At one point we'd talked Liam-cam. I'd even confided in them about the complications I was having in this pregnancy and my hospital stay in case they wanted to document it. I thought women would relate to what I was going through. But the decision had been made.

There would never be a season seven.

TORI & DEAN had been a long journey. It had started with my first pregnancy, and those cameras had witnessed the birth and growth of our family. I couldn't believe it was over. I lay in my hospital bed, trying to carry Patti's wisdom and hope into this unexpected and upsetting development. I believed that the universe had a plan for me, but I couldn't see how and why this fell into it.

Oh, and it would be a good two weeks before I heard a word directly from Oxygen. Finally, one of the heads of the network e-mailed me, saying something like, "I hope you know that was one of the hardest decisions we've had to make. You guys have been the face of the network . . . ," etc. He concluded his note by saying, "Hope your pregnancy's going great." Yeah, my pregnancy was absolutely fantastic.

I wrote him back saying, "Yes, I'm sad as well, and my pregnancy's not going great. I'm in the hospital. We discussed this as a story line so I'm surprised you didn't know." He never wrote back.

A True Renewal

Before I was pregnant with Hattie, Dean and I had gone through a real rough patch. Some of the issues we'd had were tied to Dean's bike racing. I had good reasons for not wanting him to ride. He'd been in a couple accidents, and once he'd broken his collarbone. After that I said, "This is silly. You have kids." He'd promised not to race anymore. That turned out to be a very qualified promise. He wouldn't race . . . but every other form of adventure riding was fair game.

As I mentioned, our conflict emerged on the show, and to wrap up the season on a high note, we'd decided to do the vow renewal as the season finale. To lead into it,

Dean spirited me away to Chateau La Rue, the bed-and-breakfast in Fallbrook where *Tori & Dean* began. When we moved to the inn, we'd rented it with an option to buy. We did lots of work on the house, making it our own, but the deal was that if we didn't end up buying it, we had to pay for the owner to change it back to what it was. Now, arriving back at the inn, the first thing we noticed was that the owner had kept the chocolate-brown exterior. But she'd changed lots of things back.

The reversion that broke my heart was the rose room. When we took over the inn this room had a pink carpet, pink walls, and a matching floral bedspread and curtains. It had a certain retro charm. But we redid it as our "Tiffany" room, using black, white, and Tiffany blue, with Jonathan Adler accessories. When guests weren't occupying that room, it was where baby Liam and Patsy stayed, so it held a special place in my heart. I was sad to see that the owner had re-rosed it. Nor was I convinced it was a savvy business decision.

After we were done filming for the day, Dean and I decided to drive down the coast. We ended up in a town where we'd never been before. We stopped at an old-fashioned diner and decided to sit at the counter for ice cream.

Sitting there, we started talking to the mom and pop who ran the diner. They were around seventy years old, and they'd been married for fifty-some-odd years. They had children and grandchildren. She was bubbly and cute. He was the straight man who kept throwing in his two cents. As they spoke, they started to remind me and Dean of ourselves. He said, "When she met me I rode motorcycles. She stopped that." Dean kneed me under the counter. Then she said, "He was into adventures, then it became all about family." I glanced at Dean.

He said, "She changed my life. I was on one path. But after we met, all I wanted was to spend the rest of my life with her."

Dean said, "That's how I feel about you."

They said, "We still hold hands when we walk down the street." It was really adorable.

I asked the wife, "You've been married fifty years. How do you make it work?"

She said, "Marriage takes work. It's not easy, but it's worth it."

Then her husband said, "She's always right. I figured that out a long time ago." Then he whispered, "Or I let her think she is." They reminded me of us so much that I had a sudden epiphany. It was all going to be okay. Dean and I were in a rough patch, but we were going to make it through.

As soon as we left the diner, I called our producers. I said, "We found the kicker to this story. This couple is the older version of us. We have to come film them tomorrow."

The producers said, "Tomorrow's booked. We have scenes all day."

I said, "We have to make room." The producers were into it, so they changed the next day's schedule. The new call sheet that came out that night said "T & D visit diner and get advice on marriage."

The diner encounter came just in time. I hadn't been completely sure about the timing of this renewal of our wedding vows, but I got caught up in the moment. There had to be a reason we'd met this couple right before we renewed our vows.

But that night something happened that resowed the seeds of doubt in my mind. Back at the inn, Dean sat me down in the master bedroom and said, "I hate to tell you this, but here's what we're up against. I've gotten our lawyer involved." He then proceeded to tell me that one of his biker friends had told him that another one of his biker friends had bragged about how he'd found a sex tape of us on Dean's computer, copied it, and was attempting to sell it to entertainment shows or anyone who would pay the right price.

I was horrified. I knew exactly what sex tape it was, because there was only one. There was a moment in the fourth season of *Tori & Dean* when Dean was away filming *Santa Baby 2* in Calgary. I was in New York on business with Mehran and the kids. Mehran and I were going to spend Valentine's Day together, but instead Dean surprised me. We spent Valentine's Day together. (The irony was that I never let them surprise me on the show. I hate surprises. I always said, "Please discuss it with me and I'll pretend I don't know. I'm good at faking surprise." When the network saw the footage of my Valentine's Day surprise, they responded, "This staged scene plays false. The audience will know we set it up." But it was real! Apparently my acting was more believable than my actual surprise. Take that, doubters.)

That night, after he surprised me, Dean and I had a romantic Valentine's night. Dean said, "We should tape ourselves having sex." He had a little portable tripod, and he set up his video camera on it. Afterward, I checked my angles and they were good, so I allowed him to keep it. He uploaded it to our computer at home . . . without password protection. It was just sitting there on the computer, and apparently one of his so-called friends had gotten his dirty paws on it.

Our lawyer sent this dirtbag a letter, and he didn't respond. We never heard from him again, and the incident went away. But my doubts about Dean and his motorcycle shit crept back toward the surface. I had never liked these motorcycle friends and resented that he'd brought them into our lives.

The next afternoon we sat down to film at the diner. We prepped the couple for the scene. The director said, "Tori and Dean loved hearing about your relationship. Just tell them about yourselves; tell them your stories." Dean and I got ice cream and sat across from the two of them in a booth. But as soon as the cameras started rolling, the husband got totally nervous. He could barely speak. Then he shifted gears. This was his big break. His moment. He started telling us his war stories and blurted out, "We had to kill those Japs." At some point he even used the N-word. Our sweet, romantic Dean-at-seventy was a racist dickhead! His wife tried to stop him, but he turned to her and said, "Woman, shut up. You don't know."

I tried to salvage the scene. "So how do you make your marriage work?" I asked. But he was on a rampage and she was so mad at him she was nearly in tears. The whole scene ended up on the editing-room floor. None of it was suitable for our wholesome family show. Another blow to my epiphany.

During the season, in one of our arguments about the biking, Dean had said that he was sad that it wasn't a hobby we could share. He talked about how other

bikers' wives went out on rides with them on beautiful days. In the interest of compromise, I told him that
I was open to going on a motorcycle with him, but it
would never happen in L.A. We could try it sometime
in the country, where it felt like the streets were less
crowded and safer.

The next morning, Dean appeared in his leather riding gear astride a big, white motorcycle—my updated
prince on a white stallion. He said something like, "You
promised me you'd get on a motorcycle if I took you out
of the city. Let's go." We took a beautiful ride out into
the country. A cameraman in a follow car took scenic
shots, and there was a camera mounted on the back of
the motorcycle. As the anti-motorcycle wife, I had to
admit that it was really fun—and the footage was spec-
tacular.

After our motorcycle ride, Dean brought me back to
the inn, where he had a picnic ready. We sat on the grass
in front of the gazebo with the pond behind us. There
was a long shot across the whole lawn of the B&B. Dean
surprised me by asking me for my hand again. It was a
chick-lit engagement fantasy, with Dean sweeping me
off my feet for the ultimate romantic proposal. I said yes,
of course. But at the same time I couldn't help wondering if I came across as emotional enough. Did I look in
love? The producer in me was interrupting my special

moment. Just after Dean asked me to marry him again, he let out a caw like a frightened rooster. I heard the kids' voices and turned to look across the lawn. There were Mehran, Scout, Bill, and the kids. Liam and Stella started running toward us. We ran toward them. I knew we'd edit it to play in slow motion: our family reunited. It had all come full circle back at the B&B.

I could never bring myself to watch that episode when it was finished. Those scenes bothered me because the emotion behind them was conflicted. But I saw the proposal scene in the editing room, and I have to say that that scene rocked. It was beautifully produced. I was proud of that. This was the internal struggle I had throughout the show. I'm Aaron Spelling's daughter. I knew how to write the story. I knew what would tug on heartstrings. But I was torn because it was my life we were talking about. I wanted it to be real.

That night, instead of basking in our reengagement, I had a psychic come to visit. It might sound odd, but for me having a psychic at the door is as common as a pizza delivery guy in a college dorm room. A while back, a masseuse friend of Brandy's had told us about this psychic. She lived far from L.A. and booked her sessions months in advance, but she happened to live near the inn. Brandy, Megan, and Mehran are as big psychic believers as I am. Since they were all staying with us at the inn for the filming, we had arranged for the psychic to give us a group reading in the living room.

We sat in a circle of chairs. Whoever came forth to talk about our past lives would stand (maybe hover?) behind us. The psychic could see them. Before too long, my dad appeared behind me, but this was not a shock. The psychics always see my dad.

She told us that in a previous life Mehran and I were twin sisters with blond hair and held hands skipping through a meadow. Mehran loved that. He said, "I knew I was a girl!" She told Mehran that in another past life he was not a person, more like an orb moving around. He was like, "Yes! Yes, I believe I was." We also found out that Brandy was my mother in a past life, and also a madam. Megan had some connection with American Indian heritage that took place on a reservation.

After she told us a bit about our past lives, we were allowed to ask questions about the future. Brandy, Mehran, and Megan all knew about the problems Dean and I were having. I looked at them for support. They nodded that I should go ahead. Then I said to the psychic, "Tell me about my relationship. What's the future for me and my husband? What do you see for us?"

She closed her eyes, put her hands out, thought about

it, then nodded. She said, "You won't stay with him. I don't see him as your life partner. I see that he came into your life to be the father of your children. Once that has happened you'll go your separate ways."

I asked, "How many kids am I going to have?"

She said, "Three."

I said, "I'm going to be pregnant?"

"By November of next year you'll have your third child. After that you and your husband will go your separate ways."

Dean's friend from his motorcycle world had a sex tape of us and was threatening to sell it. The charming couple at the diner hadn't panned out as the good omen I'd hoped for. My husband had just re-proposed to me and I'd said yes, but were we trying to salvage something that was already doomed? This prediction seemed like a nail in the coffin. The next day when we headed back to L.A. to plan our vow renewal, my head and heart were struggling with doubt.

TWO WEEKS LATER, it was time to film the vow renewal. As the moment approached, I didn't focus on Dean, or our relationship, or possibly scrambling to make everything right before we renewed our commitment. Instead I shifted into planning mode. It was so much easier to plan the renewal than to work on the relationship.

Production rented a house for us in the Hollywood Hills with a beautiful sunset view looking out over L.A. For the ceremony, Dean and I would stand out on a stone terrace, overlooking the view. Since we'd gotten married on the beach in Fiji, we painted a sandbox a canary yellow, filled it with sand and shells, and put it on the deck so Dean and I could stand in it, with the kids at our sides, to renew our vows.

As always, I got so caught up in the logistics, it was hard for me to make it on time to the actual event. When I was supposed to be getting my hair and makeup done, I was still busy arranging books and jars of flowers on a side table. James, who was helping me, kept saying, "Just go!" But I couldn't delegate. I didn't trust anyone else to do it my way. Mehran always says that I deal with priority number eleven before I tackle number one or two. (In this case, number one: being emotionally invested in ceremony; number two: showing up on time.)

Stella walked me down the aisle, to a song Dean and I made together, "Look How Far We've Come." Liam and Dean were waiting for us in the sandbox with all friends and family surrounding them. My mother was there. My brother and his wife had flown in for the occasion. We'd also flown Patsy in. I felt nervous and guilty. People had traveled to witness what should have been a meaningful event.

We got in position. I looked at Mario, our camera guy, and mouthed, "How's the light?" He peered around the camera, grimaced a little, and waggled his hand to say "so-so." I had taken too long, and the sun had already set. That glorious sunset was the whole reason we had rented the house. It would have looked so beautiful on camera. At least the vintage books were perfectly piled on the coffee tables and the vases of yellow dahlias on all the tables were just so.

Dean and I stood side by side. I was wearing super-high Valentino heels and had to stand with my toes clenched so I wouldn't fall over in the sandbox.

Reverend Lynn, who had done my beloved pug Mimi's funeral, was officiating. In Fiji, we had read our entire wedding ceremony from leather-bound books. Now we reenacted the exact ceremony. When we got married, I had been barefoot. This time, throughout the ceremony, I worried about the sand damaging the Valentinos.

During the vows, Liam kept trying to get Dean's attention. Dean kept putting him off. Finally Liam said, "Dad!" We saw that his pants had fallen down to his ankles. We paused the ceremony while Dean pulled Liam's pants up and of course I had to make the obvious joke about the McDermott boys not being able to keep their pants on.

Half in the moment, half imagining the scene from a director's perspective, the event wasn't magical or candid for me. As I stood looking at Dean, I checked with Mario: "Can you get both of us in the shot or should I move to the left?"

That was the romantic grand finale for season five.

IN THE SUMMER before the sixth season began, Dean decided to go dirt bike riding. At that point we still lived in Encino. Dean and two friends rented dirt bikes and went to ride them in the Malibu mountains. I was at the ear, nose, and throat doctor with a sinus infection when my phone rang. I was in with the doctor so I didn't pick up, but I glanced at the phone and saw that the caller was "babe." Dean was calling. My phone never rings. All my friends (and Dean) know that I always text.

Then a new text popped up on my phone. It was from Dean's number, but Miles, an old friend of Dean's who was visiting from Canada, had typed it. It said, "*Hey T it's Miles. I'm at the ER with Dean. Please give me a call on Dean's phone ASAP.*"

I was with my assistant Dana. When I read the text, I turned to her and said, "Ugh. Dean got into another fucking accident. I know exactly what this call's going to be. I don't even want to deal with this right now. I'll call him back when the doctor's done." I figured it was another road scrape, or they were stitching him up, and I was over it. I'd told him a million times. He did these super-dangerous sports, and this was his third accident. I was sick of this shit. I didn't want to call him back, but after about half an hour I finally did.

"Is he okay?" I asked when Miles picked up my call.

He was calm. He said, "They're just looking at his back right now to see if his back is okay."

I said, "Okay, let me know how it is. When will you guys be back?"

He said, "I think you should come here."

Then I started to get worried. I said, "Why, is he okay?"

He said, "They're just checking out his back. But you should come." He was insistent enough that I drove straight there.

When I walked into the hospital, which was in Tarzana, Miles came to meet me. He said, "I didn't want to freak you out on the phone. He's in the ICU."

Dean's lung had collapsed. He had an obtrusion on his hip with stuff embedded in it. I walked into the room. He had a tube running into his chest and a breathing mask. There was blood everywhere. He looked really fucked up. But I was so angry with him for doing this to himself, to me, and to the kids that when I walked into that room I felt nothing.

"Are you okay?" I asked.

He said, "I'm okay, babe."

I just stood there. I knew I should nurture him, but I didn't really want to.

He was dazed from the medication, but he looked up at me and said, "I'm so sorry."

I said, "It's okay. Just get better."

He said, "I promise you I am never, ever going to ride again. In fact, I'm going to sell all my bikes." I'd believe it when I saw it.

THE NEXT DAY I got the kids ready to go see Dean. Liam, who was three, was very attached to Dean. Having him gone overnight was a big deal to him. When I'd explained that Daddy was in a motorcycle accident, Liam had begged to visit him.

There were daisies growing in front of our house. On our way to the car, the kids each picked a bunch to give their father.

We arrived at the ICU and were walking down the hallway when a nurse came up to us. She said, "I'm sorry, but there are no children allowed in the intensive care unit."

At the time, Liam was a little mixed up about the familial relationships in his life. He didn't know if I was Dean's wife or sister. He always got those titles wrong. Now, when the woman told us the kids couldn't visit Dean, Liam lost it. He dropped to his knees, threw his flowers on the ground, and wailed, "Nooooooo!"

Fists clenched in the air, tears pouring down his cheeks, he screamed, "That's my son in there. I'm his wife!"

It was the funniest thing I'd ever heard. The nurse started smiling. She looked around and then said, "Okay, okay, come this way. Can you keep it to thirty minutes?"

I said, "Of course. We'll make sure nobody knows we're here." She ushered us in.

Later, I found out exactly what had happened to Dean. He and his friends were on a trail, making their way up to a place where people ride their dirt bikes. They were only going five miles an hour. He hadn't even started the dangerous part yet. Then he hit a rock, flipped the bike, and landed on a sharp rock that had collapsed his lung.

To me this accident, like the others before it, was a sign. He wasn't supposed to be doing this. Motorcycle, dirt bike, Big Wheel—I didn't care what he was riding. He kept having accidents.

Dean was in the ICU for ten days. He recovered, but we never had it out. I wanted to believe what he'd told me in the hospital. I felt bad that it had come to this, but I was glad that he now saw things my way.

Then, as season six got under way, Dean continued to ride his bikes. He claimed that he hadn't said, "I'll never ride again." Instead, he insisted he'd said, "I'm so sorry. I will never *race* again." It made no sense. He hadn't been racing when the accident happened. I was angry and disappointed.

FOR THE YEAR after that, when I was pregnant with Hattie, things hadn't been so bad. My anger had faded gradually, and we settled back into our marriage.

The same night I found out that our show had been canceled, the whole family came to visit. Liam and Stella walked in and immediately located the newest sweets I'd been given. Hattie bounced for two straight hours of pure joy in the jumper Dean set up in the doorway to my bathroom.

With a lollipop in her mouth, Stella climbed up on my bed and sat facing me.

"Mama," she said, "are you gonna make it to my birthday party?"

What? This question caught me off guard. Stella's party was a week away—a lifetime in the mind of an about-to-be-four-year-old. Was she already anticipating the disappointment she would feel when I wasn't there? This was the second blow to my heart that day, and it hurt far more than the cancellation. In my career I'd had to start over again countless times. I knew it could be done. But I had no idea whether my daughter would be forever scarred by this experience.

I wanted to be honest with Stella. After I swallowed the lump in my throat I said, "I have to ask the doctor, but probably not." I explained the reasons, in a way I thought she would understand, but she looked crushed. Then I said, "After the party, Daddy will bring you here, and we'll sneak you in to spend the night with Mommy."

"Yay!" Stella said. And just like that, the tremor left her lip and my four-year-old was back.

It was Tuesday night. This was the night Dean and I had deemed our weekly date night. The Guncles would stay at our house with the kids. We'd splurge and order two steaks from the hospital dinner menu. Dean would crawl into bed with me and we'd watch a movie on Netflix as we ate our steak dinner.

Our nanny, Paola, took the kids home, and Dean and I were alone. The news of the day had worn on me. I watched my husband as he unpacked clean clothes, snacks, and magazines for me. Day after day, he had dropped everything to be there for me and to take care of the kids, driving back and forth to see me and always coming in with a smile.

Two years earlier, Dean and I had gone through one very hard year. After that, things got better, our wounds had healed, but something had changed. Right then I realized that whatever scars had remained from my past conflicts with Dean were completely gone. His support during my hardest days showed me who he was and what we had. My husband was here with me. He was fully present. His strength showed me that we'd get through this together. It was really sexy.

I had married my soul mate and the man of my dreams. In the past years life had moved so fast that we'd both stopped finding moments to enjoy each other. I had to take responsibility for my part in this. Before this pregnancy had knocked me flat, I'd spent every waking moment moving full speed ahead. Between work, ideas, calls, meetings, and kids, there was no room left for Dean or for myself. My relationship with Dean had once been at the top of my priority list, but while his love for me had stayed constant, I'd put Dean on the back burner. When was the last time I'd given him a moment of my attention? I was stretched so thin that I felt resentful about giving time and energy to someone else. At night, when we crawled into bed, I wanted to just shut it all off.

Stuck in a hospital bed, work was barely possible. I could take calls, make decisions, design, and blog, but there was no more running from meeting to photo op to personal appearance. I was forced to rest. And the longer I lay there the more it put everything into perspective. I'd focused so much energy on work, and for what? The show was over. I should have been prioritizing my relationship the whole time.

There was a wall between us, and I'd put it there. That night, after the cancellation and the heartbreak of Stella's disappointment, I looked at Dean and that wall came crashing down. Behind it I saw him. Waiting there for me with open arms. It was Dean. The man whom I had spotted for the first time six years earlier in Ottawa on that Lifetime movie set. The lines of life and kids cradled the corners of his eyes, but it was the same handsome man whom, on a beach in Fiji with those who would judge us left miles away, I had vowed to love forever. It was the same man who, three times now, had cradled the warm bundle of a life we had created and placed it in my arms as I lay on the OR table trembling from utter amazement. He had given me love. He had given me life. He had stood by me, tall and strong, no matter how many times I ran away within myself. And now he was standing by me in sickness and in health. A fourth-anniversary vow renewal that had been carefully produced for a TV show wasn't what I needed to remind me how much I loved my husband. It took my being holed up in a hospital, flat on my back, alone most of the time, without any animals or work to distract me, to realize that Dean was my everything. Our love was so real and true—it would see me through everything else. I had fallen in love with my husband all over again.

Breaking News! Bigfoot Found!

I'd been in the hospital for a month, and I hadn't had a bleed the whole time. My fear that I would lose the baby was slowly dissipating, and I was feeling good. Also, things were happening with a new TV show I wanted to do. I'd had the idea a while back. It came from being involved in social media and meeting so many moms. I kept running into mompreneurs—these full-on carpool moms who at night, after their husbands went to sleep, were running at-home companies. The idea for the show was that I'd host a weekly mompreneur club. We'd meet to discuss our businesses and personal lives, and then the show would follow the other four moms like a smart and real *Housewives*. I'd pitched the show to a production company, Relativity. They liked it, but the right network wasn't obvious to any of us. Then Nickelodeon launched NickMom TV. From ten to midnight every night, Nickelodeon was now scheduling mom-oriented programs anchored by a talk show called *Parental Discretion*, hosted by Stefanie Wilder-Taylor, author of *Sippy Cups Are Not for Chardonnay*. They also had mom stand-up comedy and *Mom Friends Forever*, a reality show following two best friends who now had kids. I thought *Mompreneurs* would fit right into their lineup. I couldn't exactly trot out of the hospital to a pitch meeting, but Relativity was going to Nickelodeon to pitch several shows. When it came time to talk about *Mompreneurs*, they would patch me in.

An hour before they were supposed to call, I got hit by a migraine. This one was a real doozy. When I got really bad migraines in the hospital, they gave me Dilaudid, which took away the pain but also knocked me out. There was no way I could take Dilaudid right before a pitch call. I would have to wait until afterward.

I lay in my bed moaning in pain. All the lights were off, the curtains pulled. An hour ticked by, then two. I thought my head was going to explode. Fifteen minutes after the call was supposed to happen and hadn't, I decided it had probably been canceled. I accepted the shot of Dilaudid that the nurses had already prepared for me.

Seconds—literally seconds—later the phone rang.

A voice said, "Hi, Tori. We've got all the Nickelodeon executives on the line, can we patch you through?" It was Relativity.

"Sure," I said.

Nobody at Nickelodeon knew I was in the hospital. For all they knew I was in Anguilla, taking a break from surfing with Kelly Wearstler. Ha ha.

Tom, the head of Relativity, was there in the room, and he was a great storyteller. I knew he'd be able to pull off the pitch. I was just the voice on the phone. I'd chime in when necessary. But Tom said, "Tori came to us with this idea. She's the expert on it. Tori, why don't you take it from here!"

I was nearly catatonic. Dilaudid is called hospital heroin. Most people on it can't get a sentence out. I took a deep breath and started my pitch. "So . . . on Twitter I have a lot of followers who are entrepreneurial moms . . ."

Whatever I said, it must have gone well. Nickelodeon loved it and told us on the spot that they wanted to buy it.

I'm going to guess that that was the first time in Hollywood history someone sold a show from a hospital, on bed rest, on a narcotic. I know my dad would have been very proud of me for that. Talk about mompreneuring.

* * *

IT WAS THE beginning of June and I was one day away from marking my one-month anniversary at the hospital. Then I woke up at five in the morning and went to pee. As I sat up, I felt a warm gush. It was a bleed.

"No," I whispered. "No!" I had made it a month without any bleeds. The doctors had been talking about sending me home. In fact, I'd been secretly plotting to convince them to let me go to Stella's birthday party. In that instant I knew all hope was lost.

I hit the nurses' button and stumbled to the bathroom. Bright red blood ran down my leg. Bright red, I knew, meant fresh blood, and that was bad.

The nurses helped clean me up, then put me back in bed. The bleeding had stopped pretty quickly. But then, a few hours later, I had a bigger bleed. This time, sitting on the toilet, I couldn't do anything to stop the blood that gushed out of me. I was terrified. If I lost too much blood, they would have to make a transfusion and possibly deliver the baby. As the nurses tried to help me, I started crying hysterically. "I don't want to lose my baby!"

A nurse tried to calm me, but she didn't seem very hopeful. They started me on steroids, to help build the baby's lungs in case I had to deliver. When Dr. Silverman did a scan it showed that everything looked the same. The placenta had not moved—it was no better and no worse. He told me he didn't think that I would have to deliver right away and that he was hopeful that I could stay pregnant for four more weeks. If I made it to twenty-eight weeks, the baby would still be very premature, but his chance of survival without long-term effects would increase dramatically.

By the time Dean arrived, the doctors had left and I was alone. I saw his concerned face and just started bawling. My single purpose was to protect this baby, and my body wasn't cooperating.

"Why?" I said. "Why is this happening?"

Dean looked helpless. "I don't know," he said. He held my hand as I cried.

A doctor from the NICU (the neonatal intensive care unit) came in. Now that I was twenty-four weeks along, it was hospital protocol that they apprise me of the reality of my situation. (I guess before this point the baby's chances of survival were too slim.) They told me that although the baby was viable now, at twenty-four weeks, if I gave birth the baby would be a "micro-preemie." His chance of survival if I delivered today was 30 percent, and the baby would need respiratory support. He would be at risk for several other conditions. The doctor also told me that if the baby did survive, there was a chance that he would be in terrible distress. We might have to decide whether to keep my baby on life support. I couldn't imagine having to make that call. The baby could have long-term health issues, but if all went well, he could be fine.

Until then, I guess I'd only heard what I wanted to hear. When they told me that if I made it to twenty-four weeks, the baby was viable, I took it to mean that it'd be fine. But now I understood that twenty-four weeks marked the earliest point at which they would make an effort to save the baby.

After the NICU doctor left, I lay there, too scared to move.

All was quiet the rest of the day, except my nerves. I was a wreck. When Dean left in the early evening to put the kids to bed, I called Mehran. I didn't want to be alone. For the first time in my hospital stay I had a feeling that I might lose the baby, and it might be tonight.

"I'm sorry," I told Mehran, "but I'm too scared to sleep alone. Can you please come over?" Mehran, who is truly the best friend a girl could ever ask for, said he would come to the hospital right away.

That night, at three thirty A.M., I started to bleed again. I got to my commode and passed a huge blood clot the size of a giant guinea pig. It was dark red. Fortunately, at this point I was overly informed about the form and quality of the blood that came out of me—for once my overattention to my own shit had a useful application— so I knew that even though the clot was huge, the dark color meant that it was old blood, which was good.

A nurse and two residents came in and started poking at the clot and arguing about whether it was part of my placenta. I snapped a picture and sent it to Dr. J. After he texted me that I was okay, he and I started joking over text about the size of the clot. I sent him a picture of Bigfoot and said, "*They've located Bigfoot. He's in my commode.*" I've gotta hand it to Dr. J. He found this amusing—or pretended he did—at four in the morning.

Mehran and I tried to go back to sleep. When I woke up, I passed another smaller clot. This time for comparison I texted Dr. J a picture of Mr. Hankey the Christmas Poo (from *South Park*). Gallows humor? It should be called bed-rest humor.

In the next couple days I had another bleed, and when they took my blood count they found that I was now slightly anemic. If my hemoglobin level dropped one more point they would have to give me a blood transfusion. I tried to remain calm, but I could see what was happening here. We were on the road toward my baby's premature delivery—all we could do was postpone the inevitable for as long as possible in order to give the baby a chance to grow. Even Dr. Silverman seemed a bit sad and resigned. He usually kept a doctorly distance, but this time when he checked in with me, he said, "I know this is a nightmare."

With my continuing to have bleeds, Dr. Silverman

thought it was unlikely I'd make it to thirty-six weeks, which would have been considered nearly a full-term birth. Instead he thought it might help to give me a more modest goal. "Let's just get to thirty-two weeks," he said. "You can do it." I wanted to make it to his goal and beyond.

A few days later, after another major bleed, as I lay there waiting to find out if the baby and I were okay, I suddenly smelled pipe smoke coming from my left. I swear it was the same smell as my dad's pipe. I'm all about the visits from beyond, but this was insane. Never, since his death, had I felt my father's presence! I had to be imagining it. Then a nurse came in, and I asked her if she smelled some-thing.

"Yes," she said. "It smells like smoke."

As quickly as the odor came, it disappeared. Later, when I mentioned it to my brother, he said that once, when his daughter was a newborn, he went into her nursery and smelled Dad's pipe smoke.

"I had to tell him he couldn't smoke around the baby," my brother joked.

I felt completely sure that my father was there, watch-ing over me and the baby, and reassuring me that it was all going to work out right.

On Patti's visits she told me not to think about stopping the bleeding. She didn't want me to focus on the bleeding at all. Her prescription was for me to say, twice a day,

"My body is strong, healthy, peaceful, loved, empowered, and living in harmony." Dr. J thought Patti's work was total malarkey, and he didn't like the way my contractions increased when she was visiting me. He worried that they could throw me into early labor. But when his colleague Dr. Mandel came to fill in for Dr. J once when he was out of town, and I told him how much I wanted to go home, he said, "Make it happen. Envision it." Dr. Mandel told me that they'd done a study of gold-medal Olympic athletes, and many of the winners said that they had envisioned themselves up on that three-tiered platform wearing the gold medal. So I pictured myself healthy and pregnant, out in the backyard with Hattie crawling across the grass into my arms. I pictured Liam perfecting his break-dancing moves to entertain us while Stella crafted by my side. And I pictured myself holding a cherubic new baby. My psychic Fay had told me she had a dream that I had a boy with blue eyes and soft light brown curls. He was dressed in a soldier's uniform. I asked if that meant he was going to be in the military. She said, "No, it's metaphoric. It shows that he's a fighter." It gave me hope, and it also gave me inspiration for the Little Maven fall season: military-inspired jackets. But in the moment, that was beside the point. The baby I pictured looked right into my eyes and gave a happy smile that said, "We did it."

Milestones

On Stella's fourth birthday, in my hospital room, out of nowhere she said, "Remember when I was sleeping with Mama and there was blood?"

I knew what she was talking about. The bleed when I'd had to wake Stella to get Dean. Had it scarred her?

Liam said, "When? When I had a bloody nose?"

Stella said, "No, when Mama bled from her vagina and she called out, 'Stella! Can you go get Daddy?' and I did. Remember?" My heart broke for my daughter.

Liam said, "Yeah, I was two."

I said, "No, baby, that was right when Mama came to the hospital. It was a little over a month ago. I haven't been here since you were two."

Liam was oblivious, but I worried that Stella had been traumatized. She had told me that she never wanted to get married. When I asked her why, she said, "Getting married means having babies and I'm not ever having babies."

"Why?" I asked.

"I don't want to bleed," she said.

"I had three great pregnancies before this one. What's happening to me isn't going to happen to you," I told her. She wasn't convinced. I tried to remind myself that eventually she would see me completely healthy again and that we had years to work through this, but I couldn't help worrying.

When it came to Hattie, there are so many milestones in a baby's first year of life. I was really sad about missing them. One day Dean came in and said, "I want to show you what Hattie started doing this morning." He spread a blanket out on the floor and put her down on it. Hattie pushed up from her stomach and started to crawl on all fours. I was so proud, but it was bittersweet. I'd missed her first crawl, I'd missed her first words—she said "Dada" and I wasn't there. I'd missed her first tooth coming in. My littlest baby, my sweet Hattie, was growing without me. I remembered how the day before I'd come to the hospital I'd been so determined to take her swimming for the first time. It was as if I'd known that I had to grab those milestones while I could.

The hardest milestone for me to miss was Liam's graduation from preschool. It took place on a Friday in mid-June. Dean, Stella, Hattie, and Patsy were there. Also the Guncles and Grandma Jacquie. Dean and I set it up so that I would be on FaceTime for the ceremony. He would hold up his phone the whole time.

That morning my computer wasn't cooperating, so Dean and I connected by phone. A nurse came in to take my morning vitals and check on the baby at the same time the graduation was starting. She went about her business as I clutched the camera, focusing on that tiny screen.

The class of 2012 walked out. There was Liam wearing the outfit I'd picked out for him from my hospital bed: a seersucker suit and a bow tie. As soon as I saw him, I started bawling. I didn't want them to see me crying, so I turned the phone at an angle, hoping that if any of my family glanced at Dean's phone, all they would see was the blinking monitors, although my hand was shaking so hard I'm sure those monitors were just a blur to them.

Every member of the class of 2012 came up to the microphone to say what they wanted to be when they grew up. Liam said, "When I grow up I want to be a basketball player." That just made me cry even harder. When you're four years old, you believe anything's possible. I loved that he was setting really big, unattainable goals. So innocent.

I apologized to the nurse. She said, "Don't be sorry.

That's your baby. This is important." She handed me a box of tissues. I grabbed a ball of tissue and used it to muffle my cries, but this was no everyday sentimental glistening. I'd rarely cried that hard in my life, and not for a very long time. Maybe when my first pet died when I was eight . . . or when I first watched *The Bodyguard* on the night it was released. Nothing really compared to this. I was truly heartbroken.

Each child was called up to shake the teacher's hand and receive his or her diploma. This was Liam's first time walking across a stage all by himself. I was so impressed that he knew where to go when they said his name. What a big boy. He crossed that stage on my fuzzy little iPhone screen smiling so big and proud. When he got to his teacher, he didn't just hug her. He threw himself into her arms for a great big bear hug.

By the time my little graduate returned to his seat, my vision was so blurred with tears I could barely see the screen. This was Liam's beaming, proud moment, and I wasn't there.

Another nurse came in. By way of explaining my condition I said, "My son just graduated from preschool and I missed it."

She said, "This is just the first of many. You'll be there for all the rest."

"I know," I said, "but I missed this one." That was the

low point of my time on bed rest. I couldn't see the glass as half-full right then. Liam wouldn't remember or care, but I would always know that I'd missed my first baby's preschool graduation. I'd never see it. It was over. I longed to be home with my babies, making up for lost time.

There was an upside to the end of the school year, and it brightened my days immediately. Now that it was summer vacation, the kids and Dean could move closer to the hospital. We had rented a two-bedroom apartment nearby. It happened to be in the Marlowe, the same apartment building that Dean and I had lived in together when we first met. They would come to the hospital every day from now until the baby was born.

THEN, A FEW weeks later, a miracle happened. When Dr. Silverman finished scanning me carefully, he said, "We have good news here." The placenta had moved! Dr. Silverman was very pleased with what he saw. He said that if everything stayed quiet for the next few days, if everything stayed the same, I could go home.

Three days later, Dr. Silverman released me, on one condition. He wanted me to be within fifteen minutes of the hospital at all times. He said that I should stay in bed and make sure not to move around too much. He would see me in two weeks and reassess whether I could go back to our house for the rest of the pregnancy. Dean and the kids were already in the Marlowe, ten minutes away! I was all set.

After fifty-five days in the hospital, I was released. I was thirty weeks pregnant.

ALL OF US and Patsy were squished in a two-bedroom apartment. Liam and Stella slept on a mattress right next to our bed. I was happy. On the Fourth of July, we wrapped a bandage around my ankle so it looked like I'd hurt myself, and Dean put me in a wheelchair and wheeled me down to sit poolside. The Marlowe wasn't exactly a family destination. The pool was full of singles in bikinis drinking margaritas. But I sat in the sun in my wheelchair, with my fake sprained ankle, watching our kids frolic. Being free from the hospital was a great way to celebrate Independence Day. Our family was together again.

Two weeks later, when I saw Dr. Silverman again, he had more good news. The placenta had moved completely. He, and later Dr. J, was completely amazed. They'd seen placentas move slowly out of the danger zone, but never so far, so completely, so fast. It was unheard of. Dr. J actually said it was a miracle.

He told me that my pregnancy was no longer high risk.

It was completely normal. I could deliver at thirty-seven weeks. He gave me my final shot of steroids and sent me back to Westlake Village. As we left the office, Dean was pushing me in a wheelchair. Dr. J said, "You can walk out of this office." I stood up, then realized I had to lean on Dean because I was weak from bed rest. Who cared? I was going home.

During that last month of pregnancy, I decorated a nursery for the baby. I did the walls in the same bright turquoise wallpaper I'd had in my hospital room. Scout was skeptical. Did I really want a long-term reminder of my time in the hospital? I did. That wallpaper was my bright spot in the hospital. And now that it was over, I didn't see the hospital as a nightmare. I'm not an independent person, and in the hospital I was on my own for a long time. It was just me and the baby. That period had bonded us. I wanted to preserve the best of that experience, and I wanted him to see it when he was out in daylight. That paper wasn't the hospital or my high-risk pregnancy. It was us. Me and Finn (because that is what we would name him). Even now, every day when I walk into that room I look at that paper and smile, because I remember the journey we went through together and how much it means.

Dr. J told me that we had to schedule my Cesarean right away—the hospital would book up. He suggested

August 29, but as it happened I had a personal appearance—a charity event for Lunchables—scheduled for that day. It had been scheduled long ago, when we thought the baby was going to be born the third week of September. I hadn't worked for so long—I didn't want to give it up.

So now I had to pick another day. I put Patti and Fay on it, asking both of them what the most auspicious dates for this baby's birth might be. It was psychic versus psychic. They came back with September 7, but Dr. J wasn't willing to wait that long. Then they wanted September 3, but that was Labor Day. September 1 was no good—Saturdays are too busy at the hospital. August didn't seem right to me, but I had run out of options. Finally Patti and Fay told me that August 30 was the perfect day for this baby to be born. Frankly at that point I think they were just trying to make me feel better.

I made it to thirty-seven weeks. Finn was born on August 30, full term, weighing six pounds, six ounces. Liam, Stella, and Hattie came to meet him the night he was born. There were no reality cameras this time. The moment was all ours.

I'll never forget the first moments of Finn's life. They placed him in my arms and I held him close, my tears moistening his perfect new cheeks. Here was the baby boy whose image I'd envisioned for all those months. He had asked for my complete love, and I had given it. I had devoted my whole heart, soul, and body to keeping him alive, and now here he was, his little heart beating quick and strong. His fingers curled into sweet fists. A miracle. I nuzzled him and whispered, "We made it."

The Fourth Hole

Two days after I got home from the hospital, when Finn was only five days old, it was Orientation Day at Liam and Stella's new Westlake Village school. It was a small, quaint school where all the kids wore uniforms. Both kids had orientation at the same time, so I went with Stella to her new preschool class while Dean went with Liam to kindergarten.

I sat through the review of the daily schedule and pickup/drop-off procedures, but when the teacher said, "We have class parties for every holiday. You can sign up to bring food," I immediately perked up. This was my domain. There's nothing I love more than bringing home-made, theme-appropriate, kid-friendly food to a holiday party. The memory of store-bought hummus and crudité platters at the kids' former preschool still gave me nightmares, but this was the start of a new day. As soon as the teacher finished talking, I made a beeline for the sign-up sheets. I reminded myself that I had a newborn at home. Best not to overdo it. I would only sign up for Halloween and Christmas. And maybe Valentine's Day. And definitely Dr. Seuss's birthday. I mean, I had to make my green deviled eggs and ham.

I assumed the sign-up sheets would list each holiday and then give you the option to sign up for food, drinks, dessert, or paper products. That's how they'd done it at the kids' last school. To my shock, these sign-up sheets were much more specific. For the Halloween party I had to sign up for grapes, crackers, carrot sticks, juice boxes, or pizza. Those were my only options. I stared at the sign-up sheet, my mouth falling open in horror. There wasn't even a space for "other." How could I make something special? I moved over to the Christmas party sign-up sheet. It listed *exactly the same foods*. An organ struck chords of doom in the background music of my brain. No themed holiday food. The world was ending.

I shyly approached the teacher.

"Excuse me," I said. "I love baking and cooking for holiday parties. I went to sign up, but I noticed there's a specific list. Nothing homemade."

The teacher said, "Oh, we've just found that it's easier to give people guidelines."

I said, "This list is fine . . . but if I made something homemade, would that be okay?"

She said, "Of course. We love homemade. You know, if you like being involved, you could sign up to be a room parent."

Suddenly it was all clear to me. If I were a room parent, I could control all the parties. If I controlled the parties, I could make sure everything was homemade. Heck, I could make it all myself. I quickly found the room parent sign-up sheet. There were three spaces on it and two were already filled. Just in time! I put my name down. I could see the Christmas party now: A towering tree of homemade red and green French macaroons. A gingerbread house in the shape of the school with sugar stained-glass windows . . . and the wall outside this school would be built with saltwater taffy bricks that wouldn't be knocked down by a paparazzi-fleeing mom.

The minute I got home, the e-mails started. Maybe under ordinary circumstances I would have been able to manage, or politely avoid, the influx of e-mails about the various issues room parents were supposed to handle, 90 percent of which had nothing to do with innovative holiday baked goods (note to self: read the fine print). But two days after orientation, I was hit with much bigger problems.

THE C-SECTION I had for Finn was my fourth. I'd always weathered the surgery pretty well. (Too well, some might say. Thanks to my speedy recovery I now had two babies only ten months apart. You're supposed to wait until six weeks after the baby is born to have sex, but my husband has never been great at math.) Anyway, Finn's birth had gone as smoothly as the others, and afterward, in the hospital, I felt great. But soon after I came home, I was in severe pain at the site of the incision. It was far worse than anything I'd felt with the other babies. When I told Dr. J, he said, "You shouldn't be in this kind of pain." I agreed with that. Nobody should be in this kind of pain. But it sounded like he was saying "you shouldn't" as in "you *aren't*." Yet I was. Finally, I told Dr. J that I couldn't take it anymore, so two days after Liam and Stella's orientation I made an appointment to come in to see him.

Dr. J's office was a full hour away from our new house. It also happened to be relatively close to the Hotel Bel-Air, where Mehran and I were planning an event with JCPenney to launch our partnership with them for our children's clothing line, Little Maven. So naturally I coordinated the two, figuring I'd squeeze in a quick meeting with the event rental and catering companies en route to having the doctor check me out.

There was only one problem. My incision hurt so much I could barely stand up.

No matter. I arrived at the Bel-Air and hobbled down the stone path toward the bathroom. As I slowly made my way there, a man stopped me.

He said, "Hey, Tori, my wife's a big fan of yours." He was middle-aged and balding, wearing too-new jeans, cut high, and a leather aviator jacket, crisp and new. I pulled myself up straight, put on my public face, and thanked him. He asked to take my picture—or if I would say hi to his wife on the phone; my memory's a little blurry on that. I complied, and then he said, "By the way, I'm Steve Madden, the shoe designer."

I said, "Oh my God, I'm such a fan of yours. I love your shoes. I have tons of them!" In my head I was thinking, *See? It pays to be nice.* I had visions of boxes of free shoes being dropped off in my driveway.

The man I now knew was Steve Madden said, "Well, thanks a lot. See you around. Keep buying my shoes!"

No free shoes? No family-and-friends discount? Oh, well. "Bye, Steve," I chirped, and resumed my slow stagger to the bathroom.

By the time I came out of the bathroom I was walking doubled over in pain, hand on my incision site. A voice came from across the courtyard: "Hey, Tori."

It was Steve Madden. He must have reconsidered. The new fall combat boots I'd been eyeing would be mine.

Seeing my awkward, desperate, incision-clutching hobble, he asked, "What's going on down there?" and waggled a finger in the direction of my crotch.

"Nothing," I said. "I just had a baby, Steve. C-section. Recovering." I waved him off and kept hobbling.

The pain was definitely escalating. When I got back to Mehran I said, "There's definitely something wrong." He pulled up a chair for me. I sat down and took a deep breath. Then the concept for the Little Maven party came to me. In a rush, I fired off ideas. "It's Camp Little Maven. There'll be a campfire, roasted marshmallows." I was on a roll. There would be interactive stations where the kids could make friendship bracelets and pet rocks. We'd have pretend fishing in a man-made pond, where the prizes would be jars of gummy worms resting on crumbled chocolate-cake soil. Across the whole campsite would be clothing lines with old-fashioned clothespins holding the samples so people could see the collection as they walked through the party.

As soon as I finished brainstorming, the pain came

surging back. My friend Jess drove me to the doctor. I lay back on the chair and Dr. J untaped my incision.

He said, "Now I understand why you're in so much pain. It opened up."

It was open? I'd never heard of this. Dr. J said this complication wasn't common, but it could happen. While he was still examining me, I handed Jess my phone and said, "Could you take a picture for me?" I love gruesome stuff, but when I saw the photo of my incision I wanted to throw up. I guess I figured just the top layer of skin would be open. A little open. But no, it was two inches wide and two inches deep. I could see my insides. Instagram, eat your heart out. This image would definitely knock Kim Kardashian's ass off the popular page.

Dr. J said, "The good news is that it's all clean, there's no infection. But I can't sew it back up. If I do, we'll trap bacteria in there. We have to pack it with gauze. It will close up all on its own."

That was all. I had to take it easy. A nurse would come to my house daily to repack the wound. We'd keep an eye out for infection. I'd come back in a week. There was nothing to worry about. What, me worry?

At home, the nurse came every day. A couple of days we couldn't schedule the right timing with the nurses, so Dean excitedly stepped in. He put on glasses with a light attached and gloves and packed my wound. He said, "I'm not a doctor but I've played one on TV." I didn't have a choice. I'd have to trust him.

I said, "Is this gross? Do you think less of me?"

He said, "Are you kidding me? I love every part of you, insides and out. And besides, right now I can say my wife is a four-hole girl. I'm a lucky man."

Oh, babe.

Meanwhile, the room-parent e-mails for Stella's pre-school class kept rolling in. "Hey, guys, how about Wednesday after drop-off we grab coffee and discuss the harvest festival?" We room parents needed to set up the pre-K booth at the festival. We needed to man the pre-K booth in shifts throughout the festival. We needed to clean up the pre-K booth after the festival. Also, there was something called a class roster list that had to be distributed. There was a daylong e-mail chain about that. Plus the room parents had weekly meetings, which required a zillion e-mails to schedule.

Oh my God! I didn't have time for this on a normal day, much less with a gaping, probably infected wound. Man, this involved-parent thing backfired on me every time. But at least right now I had a good excuse. Things really weren't going well. I was running a fever and the pain level wasn't decreasing. Eventually, Dean took me to the ER, where the doctor diagnosed me with an infection and, upon learning I had four kids, asked me if I was a Mormon. Because there is such a big Mormon population in the San Fernando Valley.

Even with a megadose of antibiotics, I just kept getting worse. On Saturday, September 15, just two weeks after Finn was born, the home-care nurse came in to see me at three P.M. She repacked the wound as usual. It looked fine, she said, but she didn't like that I was still in so much pain. She said, "Let's keep monitoring it. I'll see you tomorrow." Then she left.

An hour and a half later I was lying in bed. Patsy was sitting at the end of the bed, holding Finn. I said, "It shouldn't be hurting this much." Then I looked down. The incision was supposed to be packed with gauze. But the packing had pushed out. A red ball was sitting on top of my skin. It looked like a shiny, hairless scrotum. Holy fuck.

"Pats, something's coming out of me!"

Patsy came over to take a look. Infinitely mellow, Patsy always talks me off the ledge, telling me everything's fine. But this time she just said, "We'd better call Dean." Carrying Finn, she left the room.

I stared down at this red golf ball on my abdomen. It was just sitting there. What was it? I was starting to freak out.

Dean is absolutely the best person to have around in

an emergency. He came into the room, looked at me, and calmly said, "It's going to be fine, but we should get you to the hospital. Let's head there now." He started to pick me up. I panicked.

"Please don't touch me! I can't go to the car! I'm scared to stand up!" I said. I was afraid that more of whatever it was—something that clearly belonged inside my body—would make its way to the outside of my body.

Dean said, "Do you want me to call an ambulance?"

I said, "Yes, call an ambulance, please. Hurry."

Within minutes, two emergency units arrived, both with lights flashing and whirling. The EMTs wheeled me on a gurney through the house and out the front door. Liam and Stella were playing on their scooters in the front yard. Now they stood and silently watched me roll by. I waved at them.

"Hi, guys!" I said. "Don't worry, I'll be back soon."

They said, "Bye, Mom!" and went back to playing.

They had seen me go to the hospital so many times it was like, *Okay, will you be home for dinner?* Just another day in their lives.

At Los Robles Hospital, when the ER doctor came in, he confirmed what Dean, Patsy, and I had all suspected. What we were seeing was part of my intestines. It was life-threatening, and it had the not-comforting term "evisceration." I would have emergency surgery at midnight.

So they pumped me up on pain meds, and I waited for surgery. Meanwhile I could hear a gurgling sound as . . . well, let's just say that within a couple hours what was emerging from my incision was no longer the size of a golf ball. Now it was a grapefruit, sitting on my belly. It was alarming. The doctor came back in and said that instead of waiting until midnight, I was going into surgery immediately.

I could see the urgency, believe me, but, as always, I asked a million questions about every aspect of the situation. Even so, I can't say that my questions make me an informed patient who understands the situation. They're just a hopeless attempt to quell my hysteria.

"For the surgery—do you do light sedation?" I asked. I'm terrified of general anesthetic.

No, he told me, it would be general for this surgery.

"But I had a bowl of chicken noodle soup!" I said. "I thought you said I couldn't be put under if I'd eaten in the last five hours."

The doctor told me that general anesthetic was protocol for this surgery.

"But why do they tell you not to eat? What can happen?"

The doctor explained that with general anesthetic, if you've eaten, there's a chance that you can throw up and aspirate. If this happens while they're inserting or removing the breathing tube, you can die.

I said, "But that could happen! I ate! I don't want to die."

I understood that I might also die if I didn't have the surgery right away, but I really thought these doctors should think outside the box. I started trying to negotiate.

"Technically, this is like having a C-section. Can't you just give me an epidural?"

"No," said the doctor. "We always put people under for this."

I could see that the doctor was trying to be patient. Dean was at my side, ready to convince me to go through with it. But I was thinking about my dad, and the story he told about when he was shot in the hand in World War II. The doctors were going to amputate two of his fingers. He said he went straight into storytelling mode. "I told them, 'I'm a pianist. It's been my lifelong dream. My parents had no money, but they found a way to send me to music school. I can't lose my fingers.'" Somehow my father convinced them to do surgery instead of amputating. They saved his fingers. They were crooked his whole life, but at least he had fingers.

My father had kept his fingers by sheer force of will. I was fighting for something much more important—my life! (Or so I saw it.)

I said, "I don't want to go under! I've eaten! I'm scared! Can you try an epidural? If there's a problem, you can put me under." The poor anesthesiologist couldn't take it anymore. He gave in and agreed to do the epidural.

The doctor had to take my intestines out, wash them off, and put them back in. As soon as he started tugging at my internal organs, the pain was intense. I felt like my insides were being pulled out of me. I started screaming. The doctor said, "I can't do this. You're moving, and you're screaming. If you keep screaming I'm going to put you under."

I clenched my fists so hard that my nails cut into my palms. I bit my lip and forced myself to stay silent. It was really, really awful.

Yeah, that epidural was a big mistake. Afterward, the doctor said, "That was bad." He admitted that if I'd been under general he would have checked around to make sure there was no other infection or issues to address. He said, "But I couldn't do that with you screaming and moving around."

I said, "I'm the patient! You let me talk you into it!" If he'd told me he couldn't do everything he needed to do, I would have let him put me under! I must have been more persuasive than I intended. Maybe I should've been a lawyer.

Sometime later, when a doctor at Cedars was looking at my records, he said, "You had an epidural for this surgery? Why did you have an epidural?"

I said, "Um . . . I convinced the doctor?"

He was shocked. He said, "It's incredibly dangerous that you were awake through this surgery. If I were doing the surgery I wouldn't have given you that option. It's not okay."

Oops.

VIP Fail

I was in Los Robles Hospital for ten days after the sur- gery. During my recovery, they gave me a Dilaudid drip, which had a button that I could push when the pain was extreme. The dose is controlled so that you never get too much, but I was still worried about taking an opiate, so I tried to get by on as little as I could. The nurses would come in and ask about my pain level. I'd say, "Pretty bad." They'd say, "Well, push the button!"

When Liam and Stella came to visit me, Liam thought that the drip button was some kind of video game. He pushed the button. I said, "Don't push that! It's my med- icine!" Stella thought this was pretty funny and started pushing the button too. I knew it wouldn't give me extra

Dilaudid, but even the unfulfilled requests for meds were monitored. I was embarrassed that the nurses would think I'd been hitting the button like a desperate addict.

Then I felt a dose of the medicine hit me. It instantly helped the pain and made my eyes feel heavy. Liam said, "Mom, why do you go like this?" He imitated me, rolling his eyes back into his head, his tongue lolling. I was horrified. How many friends and nurses had seen me like that? The next time a nurse came in I made sure to tell her the kids had been the ones to push the button. She said, "Of course they did," and I could tell she didn't believe me.

Liam, Stella, and Hattie all came to visit, but I was apart from Finn for that whole time. That was the hardest part—they change so much in those first few weeks. I had to stop breast-feeding him, and I knew that even when I went home I wouldn't be able to pick him up, much less Hattie (again!), for a long time.

The nurses drew blood every day. Though I had many lovely nurses, for some reason the ones who were responsible for taking blood had no bedside manner. They would shuffle in at the crack of dawn, grab my arm without so much as a hello, and start probing for a vein.

One morning a nurse flew in at the end of the morning shift. At some point I had a complication with the incision—an abscess—and two nurses were in the middle of explaining something about it to me. The nurse who'd come in to get blood was obviously in a rush. She snatched my arm.

"Can you wait a minute?" I said. I started to sit up, but she pushed me back down with all her might.

"You're fine!"

I gasped. The two nurses, shocked, said her name sternly.

"Whatever," she said, throwing my arm down and storming out of the room.

Now, at the hospital there was a woman in the admissions office, part of whose job seemed to be handling PR and VIP stuff. When I had arrived, she had checked in on me to make sure all was well and to reassure me that this hospital was completely discreet. To drive home her point, she had made sure to tell me that when Heather Locklear was hospitalized after a 911 call, this was where she had been admitted—and none of the staff had leaked anything. She was proud of their security . . . so why was she telling me this? Was it because all celebrities were in some elite club where secrets were safe?

Anyway, since the woman who handled VIPs had been so concerned about my experience at the hospital, I called her to report the nurse who manhandled me. She said, "I'm meeting with the board. We're going to take care of this. I'll let you know what happens." She never got back to me on that, but a couple days later she made an unexpected appearance.

While I was stuck in the hospital, I had postponed the Camp Little Maven launch party at the Hotel Bel-Air. That was easy enough to delay, but during that time frame I was also supposed to do a voice-over for Glad plastic bags. They had a hard deadline, and if I couldn't meet it, they were going to move on to someone else. Lying in my hospital bed, I texted my agent, *"I can't lose this campaign! Can't we do the voice-over in the hospital?"* I'd done something similar for *Craft Wars* when I was on bed rest.

We made arrangements, and the day of the Glad voice-over a guy showed up in my room with a microphone and an audio box. That was it—no crowds, no camera crews. But someone must have told the VIP woman that there were cameras, because just as we were getting started, she came flying into the room.

"What's going on in here?" she asked. "Are you filming your reality show? I don't know what kind of show you're making, but we don't allow that." It reminded me of the Beaver Avenue neighbor who said, "You might be making porns in there."

I told her it was just a voice-over, a PR plug for a brand, and that it was for my website. She insisted that they didn't allow filming, but I finally made her understand that we were not, in fact, filming anything.

She finally left, and at last, I was able to record my Glad spot. I played the perky host of *OMG Extra: After the Wild Life,* a mock reality series produced by Glad, starring famous wild animals. "Hi, this is your correspondent for Glad!" I chirped. "Mr. Grizz is on the loose today. Will Possum be there to stop him? Or is he back on the juice?" It was very high energy, and there I was with my sewn-up intestines and IV drip, a workaholic reality star playing a pseudo–news anchor reporting on a mock reality show. Hamlet had a play within a play. This was a send-up within a spoof within a parody. Bring on the drip.

Oh, and I never saw that VIP woman again.

WHEN I CAME home from the hospital I was like an old lady: feeble, unable to walk, and constipated from pain meds. This last condition was particularly unsettling, especially when I took a long and panic-inducing wander down the path of Google self-diagnosis. My research showed that with my post-op condition, I was at risk for bowel obstruction. And bowel obstruction could lead to sepsis, which pretty much guaranteed death. Thus informed, a bowel obstruction became my biggest fear, and I was on high alert. Dr. J, who did not see my situation as quite so dire, recommended that I try a laxative. I took one—no results—and another.

It was Mehran's birthday, September 30. He was meeting his other friends for drinks. Ordinarily I would have been there, but instead I started having diarrhea and terrible stomach pain. This was bad. Then I got chills. I called Dr. J, crying in pain.

"Could I be septic?" I asked.

Always calm, Dr. J said, "The safe thing is to go to the ER and have them do a CT scan of your intestine."

Dean, always cool as a cucumber, picked me up and carried me to the backseat of the car. I was weeping in pain. I wanted an ambulance, but Dean wanted to drive so he could make sure I went to Cedars instead of Los Robles, the hospital of the major surgery by epidural, the nurse who pushed me, and the VIP administrator who didn't like tape recorders.

We got onto the freeway. By now I was vomiting, and Dean got Dr. J on the phone again. Vomiting, I knew from my research, was the main symptom of bowel obstruction. It meant nothing could get through. My body was shutting down.

Dean said, "She's throwing up now."

Dr. J said, *"Goddamn it."* I'd never heard him have that reaction. He was always positive.

I screamed from the backseat, "Is it a bowel obstruction?"

He said, "It sounds like it could be. I want you to get to the closest hospital."

Dean pulled off the freeway and spun around. We were headed back to Los Robles.

Meanwhile, in the backseat, things were not going well. Dr. J is usually so upbeat. He breezes right past my histrionics, doing his best to keep me grounded. Now, hearing the quiet anguish in those two words, "Goddamn it," I spiraled out. Everything started spinning. For all the irrational fears that plagued me my whole life, I had never felt this level of despair. This wasn't Internet hysteria. My diagnosis was correct. This was it. I was dying.

First I called Mehran, who was at drinks for his birthday. I said, "I'm so sorry. I'm not going to make it."

He said, "Oh my God, you just had surgery. Of course I didn't expect you here."

"No," I said, "I mean I'm not going to make it. I'm dying. And I just want to tell you that I love you. Can you please call Patti and tell her to do Reiki? Tell her to pray for me. But I think it's too late. I think my body's septic. I love you." I hung up.

Then I said to Dean, "I'm sorry. I'm so sorry this happened. I can't believe I'm not going to see Liam and Stella and Hattie and Finn grow up. Please tell them how much I love them. And I love you." I could feel myself slipping away.

Dean was quiet in the front seat. Then I could swear I heard him sniffling. He was crying up there in the front seat. Dean never worries or panics. He thinks he's invincible. That's why he keeps riding motorcycles. Even Dean thought I was dying.

Dean sniffled and said, "Don't. Don't you say that. This family is nothing without you. You need to tell yourself right now that you are not dying. You are going to be fine. Believe. You have to believe." His voice was cracking and shaking. I could tell he was crying as he was talking.

He said, "Stay with me. Believe it for me. Believe it for the kids."

I could feel myself slipping away. But words can be very powerful, and what Dean said somehow sank in. Why was I accepting this? I wasn't going to die. I was going to pull through. Dean kept talking: "You have to believe you can get through this. See yourself recovering. See yourself with your kids. We're a family. Keep picturing that. Stay with me."

All of a sudden, I snapped myself out of it. I shifted from my hyperventilating, swooning state to telling myself, *He's right. He's right. Oh my God, he's right.* Patti has always told me that when I'm freaking out on an airplane I should picture myself at a happy moment in the future. Now I started picturing myself with the kids. I imagined Liam's wedding, Finn graduating from preschool, Hattie getting her driver's license, Stella being promoted to edi-

tor in chief of *Vogue*. I willed myself to be there for them.
I started to breathe again.

When we arrived at the hospital, my normally mellow
husband flew out of the car and grabbed the nearest hospital employee. From the backseat I could hear him saying, "I need a gurney. Please. My wife."

He ran up with a nurse, who was pushing a wheelchair.
Dean said, "Babe. Babe, they don't have a gurney available. We need to get you into the wheelchair."

I gestured for him to come closer and whispered, "I
can't! I shit myself. I'm too embarrassed. Tell her." I was
wearing a long lavender Ella Moss sundress, once breezy
and effortless, now befouled. It was not a pretty sight.

Dean dutifully turned to the nurse and told her why I
wouldn't get out of the car.

"Oh, don't worry," she said kindly. "I've seen everything."

The two of them transferred me to a wheelchair. The
pain was still excruciating, and I was wailing. The nurse
took our panic seriously. She pushed me toward the hospital at a full-on run, expertly maneuvering the wheelchair. She could give Dean a run for his money on the
bike track. I closed my eyes, now equally terrified of dying
from sepsis and being killed in a speeding wheelchair.

"I'm taking her to the waiting room," the nurse panted.

"She can't go to the waiting room," Dean said. "She's an
actress. She can't be seen like this."

"Okay," the nurse said. "I'm not supposed to do this, but I'll take her straight to triage."

As she said this, she rounded a tight corner at full speed, hit a curb, and I flew out of the wheelchair into the bushes.

Just then, a nasty nurse appeared (not the one who had pushed me back on the bed). She said, "She has to go through the waiting room."

Our nurse was committed to my cause. She said, "You don't understand. She's a VIP."

I was lying facedown in the bushes, shaking. My dress was shit-stained. My body contorted in pain. All I could think was, *I sure don't feel like a VIP right now.*

I DIDN'T HAVE sepsis. It was the laxatives that did me in. My system was so fucked up and tender that the laxatives inflamed it. But I was okay. Later, when I asked Dean if he'd been scared, he said, "No, not at all. I knew you'd be fine." But I knew the truth. I'd heard him crying and trying to hide it. But he'll never admit it.

Baby Steps

The first month of the kids' school had passed, during which I wasn't really cutting the mustard as a room mom for Stella's preschool class. Throughout my ordeal I had continued to receive e-mails from my co–room moms. One perk of being in the hospital was that it was a great excuse for missing meetings. Now I felt obligated to step up my game.

One of the moms recognized that I was into crafting. She started e-mailing me ideas for what we could do for the fall festival. She wanted to get clear plastic cups, draw pumpkins on them in Sharpie, and fill them with grapes. They were kind of cute—definitely better than a generic, store-bought snack. And she was really excited.

She proudly told me that she'd already bought all the plastic cups at Costco. And, PS, she'd signed us both up to set up the booth.

Cut to the day before the fall festival, when this mom got called away on business. Two weeks post-op, and I set up our booth with her husband and Dean. We handed out the plastic cups filled with grapes and Goldfish, and I made the same monster fingers that I'd made for the kids' preschool: little pizzas with green plastic monster fingers sticking in the middle. I also made monster fingers out of string cheese with green bell pepper nails sitting on a green bed of shredded-coconut grass. Of course, all the kids who visited our booth went straight for the grapes and Goldfish. I tried giving them the hard sell on the monster fingers—"It's just string cheese! You can brush the coconut off if you don't like it!"—but the consensus seemed to be that my kid-friendly, theme-appropriate, homemade treats were . . . gross. It's Halloween, people! It's supposed to be gross.

THE NEXT PARTY the room moms were responsible for throwing was Christmas. The theme was different countries uniting to celebrate the holiday. The kids were going to put on a performance—all of them wearing ponchos and singing "Feliz Navidad." I immediately wanted to find out which countries were included in the celebration and to bring in one food from each country. In order to move ahead with this idea, I had to go through an approval process for room parents. Again: There was an approval process for room parents. Beat.

I sent my plan to the room-parent-coordinating poohbah for approval. The response was quick and cutting. She wrote back, "Because in the past the parties have become competitive with some parents showboating, we now tell all room parents that for holiday parties it's minimal decoration and simple food." Competitive? Who, me? I couldn't help wondering if she'd been in touch with someone at Liam and Stella's former preschool, where I'd made a habit of overdoing it with my holiday treats (I swear the school loved it!).

Anyway, when I read that e-mail, I officially gave up. I wanted out. I'd tried to give what I had to give. Now I would leave them be with their crackers and grapes from Whole Foods. I would throw down my chic chevron flag and walk away.

IN THOSE FIRST months after surgery, I barely left the house. I was still recovering. But one night Mehran and I went to pick up dinner for the kids at Brent's Deli, which is arguably the best deli in L.A. I'd never been to the Westlake Village location before.

As we were waiting for the food, Mehran and I peeked into the back. There was a bar! They were having happy hour. I ordered wine, and they brought out pickles and little plates of food, like half of a pastrami melt or a French dip. It was a perfect combo. The thought of Dean and I socializing, going to a party, or planning a date night with another couple had no appeal for me. After being in the hospital for so long, only seeing them once or twice a week, all I wanted was to be with my kids. But this . . . this could work.

The next time Mehran and I met to go over Little Maven designs, he said, "And when we're done we can go to happy hour at Brent's."

I said, "You had me at happy hour."

Happy hour at a deli. It's the best concept ever. Mehran put it best: "It's so unchic it's chic."

HAPPY HOUR WAS a good warm-up for my return to adult life. Soon I was ready for my first night out. Dean had been on *Rachael vs. Guy* on the Food Network with Carnie Wilson. Now her band, Wilson Phillips, was performing at the Canyon Club, a supper club with big acts.

We were excited to go, and for me it promised to be a perfect reentry to the world beyond hospitals and nurseries.

The morning of the concert I had a checkup with my doctor. I went with my friend Jess. On the way home we passed an enormous yard sale. Of course I had to stop.

It was a huge sale. There was junk everywhere, but I hoped that hidden among it I might find some diamonds in the rough. At first glance I thought I was going to make a killing. Then I looked at the prices. We sell vintage coffee and candy tins at my store, InvenTORI. I usually buy them for about three dollars and at retail you mark up a hundred percent. But the tins I found at this sale cost twenty-five dollars each. It was crazy. As I looked, a train wreck of a guy started barking at an old lady.

"Hey, mama," he said. "You like glasses? See if these are your prescription! She just died last week." That was his opening line. His selling point was recent death. I perked up. I love a nutty character. Soon, as I'd hoped, he came over to where I was studying the tins.

"Which one you like?" he said.

He was young and definitely stoned. He wore slouchy jeans with underwear sticking out at the waistband and a stained baseball shirt.

"I like this one," I said, pointing at a tin with a floral pattern. "But this is a lot for it."

"At that price it's a *gift* to you," he said.

I showed him that the lid was warped so that the tin didn't close properly.

"Knew it," he said. "You're a collector."

"Why does not being able to close the lid mean I'm a collector?" I asked.

"eBay?" he said.

I decided to move on. "Do you have any milk glass?"

He said, "You know milk glass. You're a collector."

I noticed a cutesy Danish paddle. It said, "May your friends be many, your troubles few, and your sausages long."

I picked it up. "I like this," I said.

"Oh, you like your sausages long?" he said.

"Yeah," I said. I was loving this. Who was this guy?

He said, "Well, I'm sure I'm longer than your man. I'm fourteen inches. Have to wrap it around my leg and tape it in place every morning." This man was my dream. Not for his sausage, but as a producer. Where were the reality cameras when I needed them? His tins were overpriced, but his game? Priceless.

A woman, presumably his wife, came out of the house and handed him a tuna sandwich. He started eating it as he followed me around the front yard. Bits of tuna fell down the front of his shirt and rested on the ledge formed by his belly.

Jess happened to be carrying a nice vintage Chanel

quilted bag with a chain strap. The man offered to buy her bag. She asked how much he would give her for it. He studied it closely, then said, "Fifteen." I was appalled. A new Chanel bag like that would be five thousand dollars. Jess's was vintage, so of course it would be less, but at $1,500 I thought he was lowballing her. Then Jess said, "Fifteen what?"

He said, "Fifteen dollars."

Fifteen dollars! He had to be joking. I said, "It's Chanel!"

I thought this guy was hilarious, and I could have bantered with him all day, but it was too hard to buy anything from him. He drove a ridiculously hard bargain, and he kept accusing me of wanting to sell his stuff on eBay. After the fifth time, I wanted to tell him, "Dude, I'm not some eBay hack. Google me."

I ended up buying a few tins, and the Danish paddle, of course. Even more exciting than my purchases was the fact that I'd actually taken another dip into the real world. Part of why I didn't want friends to visit me in the hospital was that I'm used to telling funny little stories about my day. Stuck in the hospital, I had nothing to tell. I felt useless. I could go to the concert tonight armed with tales of Tuna Fish Shirt. Bill and Scout love estate sales. I couldn't wait to download our adventure that night over wine at Wilson Phillips.

What was I thinking? It had been so long since I'd gone to a concert that I'd forgotten what it's like. It was way too loud. I couldn't tell my story and act it out properly. I'd get my mojo back. I just had to hold on for one more day.

I Am Tori Spelling

After Finn was born, I continued to work with Patti, the Reiki healer. Lately she'd been talking to me about being my father's daughter. She said, "Everything is changing for you. You've been in transition. You're Tori Spelling. You have to claim that now. You've been shying away from it."

I cringed when she said, "You're Tori Spelling."

"I hate it when people say my full name," I said. In school and afterward I'd been ridiculed for being a rich producer's daughter. The world was convinced that the only way I could have landed my part on *90210* was through nepotism. I had always hated the notion of being

Tori Spelling and being Aaron Spelling's daughter. My
friends always called me T.

She said, "You need to move forward. You've been
stuck in the past. You've told that story for so long. But
you're ready to transition. All you need to do is tell a
new story."

What she said made sense to me. It was time for me to
become who I was destined to be.

I want to have a production company. I want to create
television. That's what I really want to do.

As soon as I'd gotten out of the hospital we'd
gone to other networks to see if we could find a new
home for *Tori & Dean*. We were open to repackaging
the show or moving in a different direction. But we got
a unanimous response across the board: We love Tori
and Dean and the family, but the show has been part of
Oxygen's brand. We don't want to take on someone else's
show.

Then I spoke to Maggie, the producer who had brought
me in on *The Mistle-Tones*. She had been my network executive at VH1 for the show *So noTORIous*. While we
were filming *The Mistle-Tones*, she said that we should do
something else together.

Maggie knew I wanted to do a half-hour sitcom. She
approached ABC Family with the idea of doing a *Kate &*

Allie–type show. They weren't crazy about that, but she floated the idea I'd had of a TV Movie of the Week called *Mystery Mom*. They loved the idea of combining a two-star female comedy with mysteries.

Maggie and I talked about a few different ideas. That night I got into bed. I was lying there, expecting to sleep, when all of a sudden all our ideas came together and I saw the vision for the show. I grabbed my iPhone off the bedside table and went to the Notes app. I wrote down the whole pitch.

The idea was that there were two female actors who had been the stars of a hit TV series in the nineties, a *Cagney & Lacey*–type show. After the show ended, their careers had stalled. One of them became a reality star, and one moved to suburbia and started a family. (Guess which one I play?) Then a huge murder goes down in their town, a mob thing. The only eyewitness is a crazy man who is obsessed with reruns of the crime show the women were once on. He has a confused understanding of reality. When the detectives are questioning him, he says that he'll tell them what happened, but only if he can tell it to the two characters from the show, who he thinks are actual crime-solvers. The detectives track the two women down and bring them back together. They get sucked into the crime, end up solving it, and decide to open a real private-investigation agency.

When I told Maggie the pitch, she loved it. We tweaked it a bit together. When we were both happy with it, we wrote up the treatment and sent it—now called *Mystery Girls*—to ABC Family. The feedback was that they loved what they read but wanted to hear a pitch. We set up a meeting with me, Maggie, my agent Ruthanne, and the heads of development at ABC Family.

Then Hurricane Sandy hit. The day before our pitch, Maggie called. She was stuck in New York, but she could phone into the meeting. Then, the morning of the meeting, Ruthanne called. She was at the ER with pneumonia. She was okay, but she clearly wouldn't make it to the meeting. It would be just me and the network, with Maggie on the phone. I'd sold my *Mompreneurs* pitch from a hospital bed on serious painkillers, but I'd never gone into a network meeting to pitch all by myself. When Ruthanne heard that Maggie wasn't in town, she said, "Let's reschedule."

I was about to agree to cancel, which nobody would have questioned, but then I changed my mind. Something told me to go through with it. I had spent two and a half months in a hospital bed, much of it alone, teaching myself to have hope. Now I summoned that confidence.

I went to the meeting. It was me, Maggie on the phone,

and three executives from ABC Family. I had come up with the idea for this show in bed, in twenty minutes max. I pitched it. They practically bought it on the spot. Patti was right. I was Aaron Spelling's daughter. Tori Spelling. I could almost say it proudly.

One Last Bad Thing

It felt like our family was finally all together, in one piece. It was our first Christmas with all five kids (Liam, Stella, Hattie, Finn, and Jack). For the past two years we'd gone to Lake Arrowhead, but now the house we'd rented there was out of our price range, so we stayed home.

Money was tight. I know that sounds odd, coming from a Spelling, but the loss of *Tori & Dean* couldn't have come at a worse time financially. My real estate compulsion had put us in serious debt. I'd worked so hard and earned so much, but I had nothing to show for it. Once I was Googling myself to find an article I'd heard was published. I typed "tori spelling" into the search field and a bunch of options came up. One of them was "tori spelling net worth." Curious, I clicked on it. Google thought I was worth fifteen million dollars. Fifteen million dollars! I didn't have one million. We had some income here and there but no savings apart from our retirement accounts.

I have a terrible habit of going into denial about my finances. I think that if I don't deal with it, then it's not real. But another part of me has always used the desperateness of my situation for motivation. When the coffers drain, I spring into action, chasing down more work. When I get hungry, I make things happen. But this time, when we'd just come through the two moves and I needed work more than ever, *Tori & Dean* was canceled. I was stuck in a hospital bed. The bills had piled up.

If I was ever going to rein in my spending, it wasn't going to happen at Christmas. I went overboard, as usual. I liked to handpick personal presents for our whole list, and it was a long list. Every year we bought presents for our families; our publicist; our agencies; our business managers and the people who work for them; our lawyers and their assistants; key people at my companies, our affiliates, and the stores where our merchandise was sold; World of Wonder; the InvenTORI staff; the babysitters, nanny, assistants, and housekeeper; my friends and their children; and Patsy's family, who were going to be with us for the holidays this year. Even though I picked out some of the presents from InvenTORI, it was still madness. We didn't start shopping for our own children until two days before Christmas, which found us running around Toys "R" Us like lunatics.

Christmas itself was nice. My mother, the Guncles, and Scout's mother, Grandma Jacquie, joined us and Patsy's family. Dean had seen a special on Italian Christmas dinners and he wanted to go Italian this year. I thought that sounded delicious, but it wasn't until the eleventh hour that we discovered we had different visions for the meal. Dean had neglected to mention that in the special he'd seen, it was an all-fish Christmas Eve dinner. But our dinner was to be served on Christmas Day. Who wanted to eat seven fish courses on Christmas Day? My fantasy involved mac and cheese, lasagna, and stuffed manicotti served family-style. We couldn't come to an agreement, so on the day before Christmas, Dean drove to the Santa Monica fish market to get fresh octopus, crab, squid, and a whole *branzino*. Meanwhile I started cooking up my multiple dishes of classic Italian comfort food. We made way too much food, as always, but it was pretty festive. Things turned out fine. I love Christmas. I live for it. But afterward I was exhausted. It was just too much.

Staying home from Lake Arrowhead left the kids feeling disappointed that we hadn't had any snow for Christmas this year. They kept saying, "It isn't a real Christmas without snow." I posted that on Twitter, my way of hinting for some resort to offer us a deal, but nobody bit, so right after Christmas I started trolling the Internet.

I did extensive research. One day I was on the computer from nine to six, as if finding a vacation condo was my full-time job. But once I'd had an idea, no matter how harebrained it might be, I was incapable of letting it go. We had to see snow for New Year's.

There were seven of us, plus Patsy to help with Finn, plus our part-time nanny, Laura, to help with the other three kids, especially Hattie. That way we'd be able to take Stella and Liam skiing. There was no way we could fly anywhere with so many people. Besides, I hate flying. We were definitely going to drive.

First I looked at Mammoth Mountain, which was only four and a half hours away, but I was too late to the game. Everything was booked, everywhere. I e-mailed my friend Jenny for advice. She told me she and her family had been to the Ritz-Carlton in Tahoe and loved it, but it too was booked. I finally found a three-bedroom condo in Squaw Valley. It wasn't the Ritz, but it would have to do. It was an eight-hour drive. We would leave the next day. Dean was totally game.

We left at six thirty in the morning. Dean used his motorcycle lift—the jack he uses to get his motorcycles to the track—to strap all of our suitcases and two kids' cots on top of the car, and we were off.

The eight-hour trip took us twelve hours, what with all those kids needing to stop to eat. And stop to pee. By the time we arrived in Tahoe, it was snowing and freezing cold, but the kids were happy.

I didn't really care about being in luxury accommodations. Who needed the Ritz? Not me. I just wanted the kids to enjoy the snow.

I lie. I totally care about luxury accommodations! The condo we were staying in had a bed that was hard and low to the ground. The TV reception was poor and we only got five channels. There was a full-service kitchen, but it only had one lonely wineglass (though, to be fair, guest services had dropped off a cardboard courtesy box with a bottle of water and five wineglasses in it).

The real kicker (and yes, I know how this sounds) was that there was no room service. With four constantly hungry little mouths, plus Jack, our growing teenager, we couldn't rely on restaurants. Morning and night we would be continually running out into the cold for food. Sure, you could argue, we had two nannies. But the fact of the matter was that I didn't usually leave the kids with the nannies. We all went everywhere together.

When I did *The Mistle-Tones* in Utah, we'd gone to Deer Valley and stayed at the St. Regis. This place was perfectly functional, but it was no St. Regis. After staying at the St. Regis and looking at the Ritz-Carlton website, well, it was going to be hard for me to stay here in the condo. Hadn't our family moved enough times in an attempt to satisfy me? I vowed to keep my mouth shut and enjoy the vacation.

The next day we planned to ski with Jack, Liam, and Stella. While I was filming in Utah, Liam and Stella had gone to ski school, but they had complained about everything. They were cold. Their hats were itchy. Their boots hurt. This time we decided they'd do better if they were with us. I remembered with a twinge of envy that the Ritz-Carlton advertised that one could "ski in, ski out" straight from the lodge. Not so in Squaw Valley. We waited until Hattie woke up from her first nap. Then we all went to the village for lunch. Hattie, who was just one, was wearing Stella's old hand-me-down cold-weather gear, which was all size two. Her mittens kept falling off, and everything else was too big. So of course we had to buy her a whole new outfit. It wasn't until Hattie's second nap that we finally headed to the ski-rental shop.

We needed boots, helmets, skis, and poles for the four who planned to ski (the three oldest kids and Dean). There was a line for each piece of equipment, and everyone had to be fitted for everything. Once we had all this stuff, we would have had to lug it up to the base of the mountain, but by the time we were done with the rentals, the lifts were already closing. We'd missed the whole day.

I wasn't supposed to carry anything, so Dean somehow carted four sets of equipment back to our condo for the night.

When we woke up the next morning, after our second night at the condo, I couldn't help myself. The words came out of my mouth as if I were possessed. I said to Dean, "Oh, babe, if the Ritz had something available, we could finish our trip there."

Dean said, "I knew it. As soon as we walked in I could tell this wouldn't work for you."

I said, "That makes me feel bad; I'm not that girl." But I was. Then I said, "It's not my fault I'm an uptown girl stuck in a midtown life." I was raised in opulence. My standards are ridiculously high. We can't afford that lifestyle, but when you grow up silver spoon it's hard to go plastic.

Dean said, "Well, let's look into it. I'll feel bad knowing you're unhappy." My husband, my enabler.

"It's just that I had a vision. I saw myself sitting on a cozy couch in front of a roaring fire drinking a cabernet while you all went skiing. The Ritz has that. I can't get it out of my head." Dean called the Ritz to see if they had anything available, but nothing had changed. They were still booked. Actually, something had changed. Now I was hell-bent on getting out of this place.

Then I remembered. When Jenny and her family had

gone to Tahoe and they had stayed at the Ritz, it was the Ritz in Northstar. It wasn't even in Squaw Valley. It was in an entirely different village in Tahoe. Maybe the problem was that we weren't in the right village! Now, in my fantasies, Northstar became the Holy Grail. It had everything that Squaw Valley lacked. Luxury hotels with room service. Family-friendly restaurants galore. Ski lifts right in town. I started Googling.

I soon discovered that the Hyatt had ski-in, ski-out residences in Northstar. And, amazingly, they had room for us. Yes! These were "residences," so we still wouldn't have room service, but at least the accommodations would be a little fancier. And we could go to the restaurant at the Ritz, which was right next door. I could fulfill my cabernet fantasy.

We called down to the concierge. There had been nothing wrong with our accommodations. I was the problem. We made the excuse that the baby was sick and we had to leave. The concierge said, "Oh, you're going home?"

I couldn't lie. I said, "Well, we're stopping at our friends' place in Northstar first." The Hyatt. My new best friends.

The Hyatt condos were really nice. When our refrigerator in Malibu broke, I'd learned that I might never be able to afford a place with Viking appliances again. When I walked in and saw that there were Viking appliances at the Hyatt, I was happy. Simple pleasures.

When we woke up the next day, in Northstar, it was the third day of our ski vacation. Dean had successfully transported all the equipment from mountain to condo to condo, so we'd already accomplished the hassle of a ski vacation, but we had yet to ski. But the Hyatt was "ski in, ski out!" We were golden.

Dean and the big kids were going to ski. Patsy, Laura, the babies, and I were going to lounge at the Ritz, and at least one of us was going to have at least one glass of cabernet. The skiers would meet us for lunch.

We bundled up all the kids (which was an *I Love Lucy* chocolate-factory scene all of its own) and went outside. The Hyatt had something called the "boot valet," where the skiers in our party would leave their boots while they were out on the mountain. It was there that Dean found out we needed lift tickets—which were only available down at the village. Dean went to buy them while we all waited at the boot valet for what seemed like an hour.

There were signs guiding us to "ski in, ski out." Lots of signs. They eventually led us to a gondola, which took us to the Ritz, where the ski in, ski out actually went down. That was the Hyatt's "ski in, ski out." The Ritz. This little jaunt might have been an easy detour for a normal family, but we had the two babies in a double stroller, two little children, and four sets of ski equipment. For us it was a major hike.

Patsy had never been skiing before. When she saw the gondola, she said, "It doesn't stop!" In a frantic, stroller-jamming jumble of poles and limbs, we hurled ourselves into two gondolas and up to the Ritz.

At last the skiers went off. Patsy, Laura, and I went into the bar lounge with the two babies. We found a booth near the fireplace and unbundled everyone, making a pile of hats, mittens, scarves, and parkas. I could already taste my soup and glass of wine. I ordered the corn chowder. They were out of corn chowder. Did they have any other soup? No, they had no soup. This was the Ritz! I had no place to go from here. I ordered the cheese plate instead of the soup. Who cared? They had wine. That was all that mattered.

The waiter brought our order, but before I took the first sip, a fire alarm went off. A fire! At the Ritz! We had to get the babies out of there! At first, the waiter reassured us, saying, "Don't worry about it. Just stay seated." The fire—the intentional one in the fireplace—was so warm and pretty . . . but the piercing fire alarm blared on. All the faith I'd put in the Ritz started to drain out of me.

Two minutes later we were evacuated. Leaving our lunch behind (at least I had no soup to get cold), we put all of our clothes back on and hurried outside. Ritz staff ran back and forth. Our dedicated waiter did show up with my wine on a silver tray, and I snuck little sips as the fire alarm screamed and the babies cried. We waited. When we filed back in at last, I said to Patsy, "Everything is going wrong on this trip. Not really bad things, just one little thing after another." I had no idea how bad it was going to get.

WE'D NEGLECTED TO book a restaurant for New Year's Eve. Even though we were eating early for the kids, everything was booked. The only place that still had room for a party our size was a local sushi restaurant. We all got dressed up. Stella and Hattie wore matching velvet Harajuku dresses from Target with vintage sequined berets. Finn was in a Little Maven onesie tux. And Liam wore skinny velvet pants and a blazer with a festive sweater underneath. We wheeled the double stroller through the snow to the restaurant. You know you're in trouble when your sushi restaurant doubles as a sports bar, complete with big-screen TVs on the walls. It was loud and chaotic. The kids were about to fall apart. We sped through our meal, but I managed to down two bottles of sake (they're so small!). By the time we came out of the restaurant, I was feeling a little festive and hoping to put an end to the nightmares of 2012.

With two kids done with diapers, someone always has

to go to the bathroom. While Dean and Jack saw the rest of the group back to our hotel, Liam, Stella, and I made our way through the packed village streets, trying to find a public bathroom. As we came out of the bathroom, we saw that there was an ice-skating rink in the middle of town. Perfect! What a picturesque, magical way to end the night, my recovery be damned! We'd all rent skates. It would be unforgettable.

"Hey, guys, want to go skating?" I asked Liam and Stella. Indeed they did. It was a plan. We wiggled into the crowded rental shack. I was carrying all the skates when someone asked to take a picture with me. You couldn't move, it was so packed. "Sure," I said, and then it began. A bunch of other people wanted pictures with me. "Of course, of course," I said, smiling and posing as we kept making our way to a bench. As I struggled to get the kids in their skates, a man came up to me and said, "Can you just take a picture with my wife? Please? I'd do anything for you."

Music to my ears. I said, "Will you help me lace up my kids' skates?" It was a deal. I decided I should hang a sign around my neck: WILL TAKE PICTURES FOR CHILD CARE.

As we staggered to the rink, Dean and Jack found us.

"What are you doing?" Dean asked. It was probably only eight thirty at night, but it felt like midnight. We'd had such a long day. The kids were exhausted. We should have wandered back to the hotel and cut our losses.

He was right. I grimaced. "It was a bad idea." We couldn't turn back now. Stella and Liam were all in.

As soon as I got on the ice I realized what a mistake I'd made. I had barely walked a block since the surgery and now I was attempting a sake-fueled jaunt on slippery, crowded ice. I had no stomach muscles to speak of. One false move and I was a goner. Terrified to move, I clung to the side of the rink. Jack held my other arm, keeping me up. He was slightly amused by the spectacle and kept asking if I was drunk. But the truth was my nervousness completely overrode my buzz. As soon as the kids had their fill, we made a beeline back to our cozy hotel room. We put the kids down, and Dean turned on the TV. There was a "news" report that Kim Kardashian was pregnant. It was the highlight of the night. Happy 2013.

On New Year's Day, all the kids wanted to do was go sledding. We drove around Northstar looking for a hill, but the only decent slope we found had a sign on it: NO SLEDDING. At last we found a short, sloped driveway. What did my California kids know about sledding? That little patch of snow was all they needed in the world. So much for our luxury ski vacation. We could have stayed home, fired up the ice maker for a few hours, and called it a blizzard.

* * *

AT DINNER THAT night, Hattie was fussing in Dean's arms. I felt her forehead. She was warm, so we headed straight back to the room. On the way, Dean peeled off to get some juice for the kids from the market in town.

At the Hyatt, as we headed up in the elevator, I looked down at Hattie. She was staring up. My mother's instinct told me something was wrong.

I said, "She's having a seizure." And she was. Right there in the elevator, she turned blue. Her eyes rolled back in her head. She was unresponsive. Liam had had a febrile seizure when he was her age, so I had some hope that I knew what was going on. I said, "We've got to get her clothes off and bring the fever down."

The elevator stopped at our floor and we all piled out in the hallway. I instructed Laura to take off all of Hattie's clothes and to lay her down. Then I tried to call 911. I had no cell service. Damn it. I was sure they had cell service at the Ritz.

Our room was at the other end of the hotel. Instead, I went straight to the lobby and ran out of the elevator yelling, "Call 911, my baby's not breathing!" The woman at the desk started making the call.

The lobby was a two-story atrium. When I asked for help, out of the corner of my eye I saw feet going up the stairs turn and stop. A woman said, "My friend's a pediatric neurologist!" I ran up the stairs four at a time, the first time I'd run since my operation. I flashed back to Liam's febrile seizure, when, pregnant with Stella, I'd run down the stairs four at a time to call 911 for him.

The doctor joined me and we went up to Hattie. As the doors opened, we saw that she'd thrown up but was starting to come around. The doctor took her pulse, and as he did the EMTs arrived, and Dean was close behind them.

Hattie's blood pressure was still very low, so we headed to the hospital. The EMTs gestured me forward to ride in the ambulance with her. I lay down and strapped her to me, just as I had when Liam had his seizure. As we drove to the hospital I was thinking about how much time I'd missed with Hattie. I'd had to stop picking her up when she was four months old because of the bleeding. Three months after that I left to be on bed rest. I wasn't around for her first words or her first crawl. Throughout my pregnancy with Finn, whenever I wanted to hold her, I'd fake it with someone else standing behind her, supporting her weight. She didn't know the difference, but I did. To this day I still wasn't supposed to hold her while standing up. Missing the bonding with Hattie was a devastating loss that I worried was permanent. She was only attached to Dean and seemed to have no attachment to me. Most of the time when I reached for her, she turned away. I knew she would have been more comforted at that moment if Dean were with her instead of me. But the EMTs had assumed she wanted her mother.

I was so worried that she'd be like, *Who is this woman? Get her off me.* Instead, as we lay there together, she cuddled with me, looking into my eyes.

At the hospital they found that her temperature was still high and her ears were very infected. She hadn't even complained! They put her on antibiotics and sent us home, telling me to make sure she took a fever reducer every three hours. Once Hattie was fine, I texted Laura to ask if Liam and Stella were okay. I was worried that they'd seen Hattie go through that. Laura said that they were fine.

Back at the hotel, Stella said, "Hattie's eyes rolled back in her head."

I said, "That was pretty scary but you guys did great."

As we got the kids ready for bed, Laura said, "You were great tonight. You were so calm. I'm not sure I could do that." It may have been the first time in my life anyone ever described me as calm. But Dean wasn't there. I had to be in charge, so I acted. I made things happen. It was nice to realize that when push came to shove, I didn't panic. I felt strong.

Dean went to sleep with Liam and Stella in the living room. Hattie stayed in bed with me all night. At times she'd wake up, grab her blankie, and nuzzle in with me. It was a real moment for us. As afraid as I had been in that elevator, once Hattie was out of the woods, I saw the silver lining of that dark, scary cloud. It was our first real bonding moment. At the hospital, when they were hooking her up to the EKG, Dean had picked her up and she'd turned and reached for me. She'd always been a daddy's girl, but now I was the one holding her. I thought, *Oh my God, she wants me!* She's my daughter. I gave birth to her, but I was always wondering if I fit into her world. Now I had my answer.

The next day, when we came out of our room to go to breakfast, Liam stopped right outside the elevator. He said, "This is the area where Hattie had her disease."

WE ARE NEVER going back to Tahoe. We were so excited. All we wanted was to relax and start the New Year on a less dramatic note. To have Hattie's seizure on New Year's Day . . . I decided not to take it as a sign. I told myself it was just the residue of 2012 that had to be dispelled. It was the last bad thing, and buried in it was the smaller but life-changing joy of connecting with my daughter. I was full of hope for 2013.

Tori's Post-Baby Bikini Bod

Like any postpartum mom, I wanted to get back to my fighting weight. I'd had it pretty easy after Liam and Stella, but I never got back into shape after Hattie was born because I got pregnant right away. And went on bed rest. With the complications after Finn's birth, I didn't worry about how I looked until I felt like I had my strength back.

For several months I couldn't really exercise. There were a couple reasons. First, there was some risk that my scar would open up again. I was terrified of that. Second, I really don't exercise much, period. So I took off my weight the old-fashioned way. I like to call it the Just Keep Your Fucking Mouth Shut and Eat Air diet. It's all the rage.

I love to eat. But I nibbled rice cakes and ate soup and had dinners that looked like they belonged in some health magazine. With my sedentary lifestyle, it was the only way, and it worked. My clothes were starting to fit again.

Us Weekly saw me out and about and noticed that I was getting trim. They called my publicist saying they wanted to do a shoot of me in a bikini. We agreed, but I wanted to wait a bit. I looked okay in clothing but I wasn't remotely toned. But the magazine wanted to "scoop" the story, so we agreed that I would do the shoot two weeks later. Time to get my workout on.

Finn was seven months old. I hadn't exercised for two years (and even then I only did it to lose baby weight). My body was finally my own again. I went whole hog. That first week I had two personal-training sessions. And Dean had just gotten into MMA (mixed martial arts). It was a safe version of wrestling that the whole family could do at a gym near our house.

Dean was very excited, and when Dean is excited, he buys gear. He ordered MMA outfits for all of us. Mine consisted of dorky silk shorts, a tank top, and gloves, all in pink. I love pink, but this was a bit much. I sent a picture of myself in MMA gear to Scout, Bill, and Mehran, knowing they'd be amused. But Scout was concerned. He texted, *"a week ago you had intense abdominal pain and now you're doing this? don't you think it's extreme?"*

Brotherly love!

Finn's got swag!

Dear Martha: You crushed my
dreams . . . so now I must take
you down! Love, Tori.
P.S. I still worship you!

My four water babes.

Our traditional family foot shot. We are now complete!

Courtesy of ElizabethMessina.com

My complete family!

Me and my
backyard farm.

Doing belly shots
and photobombed
by a pig.

My true love.

My dad would've been proud
of the woman and mom
his baby girl has become.

Me and my first baby!
They grow so fast.

I can't believe my stepson, Jack,
towers over me. #IFeelOld

My very own rock band!

Just a farm girl at heart.

"It's been seven months!" I wrote back. I wanted to have control of my body again.

"Try hiking," Scout said.

I told him that the doctor had approved my activities and that the trainer knew what he was doing, but Scout was having none of it.

Three days later I was back at the hospital. Nothing had bothered me while I was working out, but over time the pain in my abdomen became severe. Scout was right. Should've hiked.

Looking at my CT scan, the surgeon said he didn't think I had a hernia. He couldn't tell, but he thought the problem was scar tissue pinching a nerve. Then he examined me. As soon as he saw the bulge of flesh over my scar, he told me I needed surgery to fix the bulge. He said, "I want to do this with a plastic surgeon."

I said, "What? Why a plastic surgeon?"

He said, "In layman's terms, it's a tummy tuck."

I said, "I don't need that!"

He said, "Trust me, you're going to want it."

Was he saying I needed it for medical reasons or that I had to have it? I couldn't tell.

I said, "I don't care what I look like."

It was true. I just wanted the pain to go away. I was happy with how I looked. And I didn't want plastic surgery—I didn't want to spend more time away from my children for vanity. And in the back of my head I didn't want to have people thinking I'd resorted to surgery to get my body back.

The surgeon said that he had to fix the scar tissue. If I didn't have surgery on the bulge at the same time, it would only get worse.

As I walked out of his office, a nurse said, "You need to know that he's a very conservative doctor. He doesn't usually recommend surgery." Still, I resolved to get a few more opinions.

Meanwhile, the fine-tuning I'd wanted from working out hadn't happened, and the bikini shoot was only a week away. I'm not interested in a tummy tuck, but I'm not completely un-vain.

I turned to slimming wraps. This fell wholly into the category of unscientific weight loss. I went to a place in my neighborhood called Suddenly Slimmer. They claimed that by wrapping my body in mineral bandages I would lose inches and my skin would tighten right up. It seemed unlikely, but at least it was noninvasive.

I used the name "Victoria McDermott" when I booked the appointment, but the woman at the desk said, "Wait a minute! I know who you are. At first I didn't know, but now I totally know who you are." She led me to a room where I was to sit for an hour, naked except for the Ace bandages that wrapped my body.

I went for two treatments, and the second time I brought Stella. There was a mini-trampoline in the room, and she bounced happily as I lay there getting what I told her was something to help my skin. We'd only been there twenty minutes or so when the same wrap lady popped into the room. "Hi, Tori! There's a woman here for a treatment. She's really excited that you're here too! She loves your show. She's never had the treatment before and she's nervous. Can she come in to meet you? You can tell her about it."

I guess she saw people naked except for mineral wraps all day long and didn't think it would be weird for me to meet someone while lying mummified on a vibrating recliner. I'm such a wimp. "Sure," I said. Fuck me.

The woman came in: "Oh my God, Tori! It's so nice to meet you."

I tried to wave a zombie hand but could barely move. "This is awkward, but hi, how are you?"

She laughed, and then seemed to get how embarrassed I was and made a quick exit.

I took a picture of Stella jumping on the trampoline and my mummified feet and sent it to my publicist with a note saying, "Gotta do what you gotta do. With my luck Stella will tell someone from *Us Weekly* about this tomorrow."

For the *Us Weekly* photo shoot the next day, my publicist had given me clear instructions as to what I should say about my weight loss. Women didn't want to know that I had lost weight through dieting, not exercising. I didn't want to be the asshole who didn't work for it. So I said that I swam. It was sort of a bad choice. I can't do much more than doggy-paddle.

Stella, who had witnessed the mineral wraps, almost blew my cover. She was in the kitchen with the makeup and hair person from *Us* before I came in. When I entered, the woman said, "Oh my God, Stella told me all about the trampoline."

"Oh, yes, I took her to a trampoline place," I said, covering.

"You got your skin tightened there!" Stella chimed in.

"It was a great facial later that day," I said. If I wasn't careful Stella would land her own feature: "Tori's Toddler Exposes Her Secrets."

Even after the shoot, I wanted to stay diligent about my diet. I stayed away from sugar and didn't take a single lick of the kids' ice-cream cones. But one night Dean and I were in bed. My Ambien was just kicking in when we heard a loud thump. We went outside and found that two of our chickens were missing. Just gone, presumed dead. One of the ones that died was a favorite of mine that we'd named Elizabeth Taylor. Their coop door was busted open. We hadn't heard any squawking, but we'd been told that there were raccoons on our property. I was devastated. Thank God Coco was safe in her dog bed in our room. She doesn't know that she's a chicken.

When we came back into the kitchen—maybe the Ambien was to blame—for the first time in my life I did stress eating. Sitting on the counter were brownies left over from the craft services at the *Us Weekly* shoot. After the shoot, as a pat on the back, I'd taken a single bite, but then Patsy said, "I see you're off your diet." I felt guilty and spit it out immediately. The night Elizabeth Taylor died, I ate the entire container of brownies.

Dean had never seen me eat like that. He said, "What are you doing?"

I said, "I'm stress eating!"

He stared at me, still not understanding.

"The chickens are dead!" I yelled, shoving the last brownie into my mouth. As Dean gently led me back to the bedroom, I realized I finally understood what the whole emotional-eating thing was all about. Our chickens were gone, but wow, those brownies were good.

Somewhere That's Green

On Valentine's Day I was in the kitchen baking treats with Liam, Stella, and Laura. I had four projects going: Rice Krispies Treats, cakes, cake pops, and cookies. Finn and Patsy were in their room. Hattie was already asleep for the night. The kitchen in our Westlake house was all windows on one side. They let in tons of sun during the day, but as the sun set, the glare made it hard to see anything but your own reflection. I pulled a batch of cookies out of the oven, and then I saw Laura's face go white. Had my cookies burned?

I said, "What is it? The cookies?"

"No, nothing. I don't know," she said. Then, after a moment, she said, "I saw someone in the backyard walking past the window."

"Oh, no," I said. "That always happens to me. You're seeing your own reflection in the window."

"No," she said insistently. "Someone walked by. They were light."

"They were light?" I didn't know what she meant.

"We're all wearing dark tops. It was a man. He was wearing a long-sleeved khaki jacket." She was stumbling over her words, but this was starting to make some sense: I was wearing black and she was wearing navy blue.

I said, "Really? What do we do?"

She said, "I think we should call the front gate." That was a good idea. This was, after all, a gated community. Surely if we had a trespasser the front gate would handle it.

Laura called the front gate. She told them what she'd seen. The guard said, "Sorry, we can't help you. You'll have to call the police."

Laura said, "But we're three women alone with four babies. Can you come up here while we wait for the police?"

The guard said, "Sorry, but we aren't armed, and we can't go on private property." He gave her the number of the sheriff's department.

Then it started to hit me. What if this was for real? What if there was an intruder on the property and we were in danger at this very minute? None of the doors were locked. The sliding glass doors in the kitchen and our bedroom had doggie doors that interfered with the lock. Some of the doors didn't even have locks. Dean had a gun but I didn't know where it was.

"Okay, guys," I said. "Let's go somewhere safe until the police are here." Laura grabbed the kitchen timer (after all, I had two red velvet heart cakes in the oven). We went out in the hallway, where we had a good view of the whole house, but I couldn't figure out a safe place to go from there. The four of us stayed in the hall for fifteen minutes, waiting for the police. We knew because we had the timer. My cakes would be done in five minutes. I called the sheriff's department again. This time the guy who answered the phone was snippy.

"I just talked to you. They're on their way."

I said, "We're alone with young children, baking and scared. Please don't talk to me like that."

He agreed to stay on the phone with me until help arrived. All of a sudden the timer went off.

The cakes! Laura and I locked eyes, panicked. "They're going to burn!" I said. I was scared to go back into the kitchen, but I couldn't send my bubbly blond babysitter. You know how these things go. The cute babysitter always dies first. I had to go get my red velvet cakes. But what if the guy was in the kitchen? Could I grab them and grab a knife at the same time? I made a decision. I had to go in. For the love of baking.

The guy was still on the phone. He said, "The cops are on your property."

I said, "They're not! Nobody's here. But I smell red velvet burning!"

He said, "I don't know why they haven't rung the doorbell."

I knew why. They were dead in our backyard.

Then the guy on the phone said, "Okay, the cops are in your backyard."

Laura and I led the kids to the back door. I saw flashlights bobbing around. I opened the door and two cops came in.

"I'm so glad you're here," I said, putting on my oven mitts as I ran to take out my cakes. In addition to the two red velvet heart cakes, I had two regular cakes that I was going to use for push pops ready to go in the oven. The cop came in to tell me they hadn't found anyone on the property and to ask me a few questions.

"Tell me about the security here," the cop said.

I said, "Hold on, I'm going to put my other two cakes in the oven." I had my priorities straight. The cakes for the push-pop cakes went in the oven. Then I told the cop that none of the sliding doors worked, and the front door was unlocked.

"Do you know how unsafe this is?"

I said, "It's a guard-gated community."

He said, "Please. They get in here all the time." We called the owners of the house, who said they didn't have anyone scheduled to do any work. The cops hadn't seen any footprints, but that didn't mean anything. They filed a report, and then one of them said to me, "I would call the security situation here unlivable. I don't know how you sleep a wink at night."

Dean was out of town on business, due to arrive back that evening. But I wasn't about to keep my family in this high-risk situation. We couldn't stay in the would-be crime scene. I gave the cops some of my fondant-coated conversation-heart Rice Krispies Treats (they came out perfectly). As they enjoyed them, I packed up all the kids and the dogs and Coco so we could check in to the local Hyatt. The cops seemed a little surprised that we were leaving.

"You just told me the place was unlivable," I said.

"Next time we can be here faster," the cop said. "I wouldn't go to a hotel."

But there was no stopping me now. I had room service on my mind.

When Dean's plane landed, my string of increasingly panicked texts came through. He read through to the bottom, which told him to meet us at the Hyatt. When he arrived, he was less than convinced about the imminent danger we'd been in.

"But the cop said the security situation was 'unlivable'!" I said.

"Come on," Dean said. "He was being a little extreme." He told me that the front door had a working dead bolt and that he could easily fix the sliding doors. I wasn't reassured.

That night, a thought that had been floating around my brain came to rest. It was happening again. We had to move. It wasn't the intruder. All he did was provoke a temporary anxiety. But we'd been renting this overpriced house for almost a year and it was time to assess our situation. The children weren't happy at the nearby school, and the best school we'd found for them was forty-five minutes away. We'd driven that far from Malibu to their preschool, and we knew it was hard on them. Above all, we had to downsize our lives. Our money manager insisted on it.

On the other hand, were we really going to move again? This was the ninth place Dean and I had lived in seven years together, and our homes were all over the place. We weren't narrowing down where we belonged and how we wanted to live. What was I looking for in all these new houses? I had a notion of a home that would complete me, complete our family, and I kept thinking I'd found it, but I was never happy. I wanted a stable life. I want something permanent. I needed that. My family needed that. But what if I never found it? I didn't want to chase an impossible dream.

What was home? I always flashed to the movie *Little Shop of Horrors*. Audrey is a trampy girl who dreams about a life different from hers. She sings "Somewhere That's Green" about wanting to cook like Betty Crocker and look like Donna Reed. Her fantasy is a little more modest than mine, but the feeling is the same. And really, there is something about the simplicity she describes that I long for.

I grew up in great luxury, wanting a simple, cozy life. Now I'm torn between the two. I have a vision of waking up in the morning, wrapping myself in a big cable-knit cardigan, putting on my wellies, and flinging open the front door. The kids run in with freshly laid eggs. Dean is on a tractor. I bring him a cup of coffee, baby on one hip. I hand it to him and go back inside. But in the fantasy of this "simple" life, we're running a farm . . . but we're still producers. My wellies are designer. The cardigan is a thick cashmere sweater-coat. And Dean's got a pimped-out tractor. The house I go inside is our super-cute "pseudo" farmhouse. It has been updated with all the latest amenities. No rough floors; only Viking appliances.

It's no mystery why I have money problems. I grew

up rich beyond anyone's dreams. I never knew anything else. Even when I try to embrace a simpler lifestyle, I can't seem to let go of my expensive tastes. Even when my tastes aren't fancy, they're still costly. I moved houses to simplify my life but lost almost a million dollars along the way for what turned out to be a mistake.

Our store, InvenTORI, had turned out to be a money pit. We invested hundreds of thousands of dollars remodeling, stocking the store with vintage finds, and paying the employees. Not only were we paying rent and staff, but I was buying estate pieces for the store and keeping half of them for myself. But did the people who visited the store buy our three-thousand-dollar couches? No. They'd walk in and say, "We saw the store on the show. Is Tori here today?" Then they'd walk out with a scented candle. Our business manager said, "You can't make money selling candles alone." The rest of my businesses were also in start-up mode. Just because I'm appearing on HSN to sell my jewelry doesn't mean it's profitable yet.

Then there were my parties—when Oxygen funded the parties I had a huge budget. But when we had non-Oxygen parties, I felt like I had to live up to the standard I'd set. We were overstaffed. And then there was my little shopping problem. I bought ridiculous amounts of stuff for the kids: clothing, toys, crafts. We traveled (and did crazy things like upgrading hotels at my instigation). Yesterday I went into a gas station to get the kids some water and I dropped fifty dollars on some DVDs (they were on sale!), chips, and some lottery tickets (because winning the Powerball jackpot might be my only hope). Patsy always says I'm the only person she knows who can walk into a ninety-nine-cent store and spend over a hundred dollars.

I can't afford to live like this anymore. Our circumstances have changed. In between the moves, the store, spending a year in and out of the hospital, and *Tori & Dean* being canceled, our bank account has taken a major hit. I can't keep chasing the grand lifestyle I grew up with. I have children to think of, their educations, and our lives together. When I'm flying by the seat of my pants, there's a cost to all of us. The more I have to work to afford the luxuries I think our family should have, the less available I am for my kids. I worry that I could look up and find that their childhoods are gone.

It's gotten so bad that our money manager is involved in every decision we make. Dean was thinking about getting a vasectomy. The idea freaked me out, but he said, "We have four kids, you want more?"

I said, "What if? What if they're out of diapers and we decide we want more?" Then friends of ours mentioned a doctor who supposedly was king of the reversible vasectomy. He was the best. But (of course) he was expensive.

Dean and I went to see the doctor and had a good

meeting. Dean wanted it done, and the sooner the better, since it wouldn't take effect for a month.

We e-mailed our business manager, but she said, "You can't afford this."

Dean said, "If T were to get pregnant again, it could be life-threatening!"

She said, "Do what other people do. Use protection." Things were really bad. Next thing you know our business manager was going to tell us to buy the cheap condoms.

They say admitting the problem is the first step. I looked around our nine-thousand-square-foot rental in Westlake Village and felt like I was living a lie. We simply couldn't afford it. The only answer was to move again.

We found a smaller house, in a less expensive neighborhood, for half the rent. The owner had very . . . *specific* taste. There were sponge-painted walls and the dining room wallpaper had hand-stitched ribbon woven into a latticework, with bows and dangling ribbons. It wasn't my dream house. But it was a house we could afford. I promised myself, and Dean, and the children, that no matter where we landed, I would make that home.

CONCLUSION:

Biting the Bullet

It is the hardest thing in the world for me to ask my mother for money. I can't stand the idea that I need help. But when it became clear that we might not be able to afford private school for Liam and Stella, I felt that they shouldn't suffer because of my mistakes. Or my unwillingness to suffer humiliation. So I bit the bullet and e-mailed my mother. I asked her if she'd be willing to contribute to the children's school. She said we should go to lunch and talk about it.

I was incredibly nervous about the lunch, but I kept telling myself that if she said no to my request, that was okay. I would just take the opportunity to have a nice lunch with her. As soon as we sat down, she said that she wanted to talk about some unfinished business. Then she said, "I'm not mad, but I want to know why you haven't paid back the money you owe me." She was right. As soon as we sold our house in Encino, we were supposed to pay her back the money she loaned us for Malibu. What she didn't know, because I had never told her, was that we sold Encino at such a loss that there was no money to pay her back. I came clean with her. I told her about that, and I told her the sad state of our affairs.

She took it very well. She was supportive and offered some advice. I didn't slip into the helpless baby manner-isms that emerge when I'm overwhelmed. I behaved, for once in my life, like an adult. And I felt like she treated me like an equal. This was a major step for us.

She started talking about how she would give us some help, and that she'd like us to continue to contribute what we were already paying for their school. But while she was saying this, I had already changed direction, saying, "I actually decided I want to try to do this myself. If I'm up against the wall, I'll come to you. But right now we're going to try to do it. But I still wanted us to have a nice lunch."

I was so determined to show that I didn't need her help that I declined it before I knew what I was doing. There were a million and one reasons I should have accepted her help, but pride stood in my way.

I failed to go through with my request for money, but in a bigger way the lunch was a surprising success. It felt like I was talking to a girlfriend. At some point my mother asked, "Why do you keep moving houses and keep getting animals? What are you searching for?" but she kept checking to make sure she wasn't crossing a boundary. I saw how careful she was being and realized that she was afraid that whatever she did would be wrong. It wasn't that she didn't care about me. She didn't know how to talk to me. That made two of us. We didn't understand each other. I had never seen it that way before. Finding common ground would take work. Maybe we could do it. I tried to give her honest answers and, for once, to listen to her advice.

That night my mother e-mailed me. She said, "I'm proud of you. I saw a whole new daughter today."

DEAN STILL GOES to the track to race every once in a while, although with me out of commission for such a long time, he couldn't justify it. One morning, when I was finally feeling better, he said to me, "I might go to the track this weekend. Are you okay with that? Can I go?"

I said, "What do you mean 'can I go'? You can do what you want."

He said, "I'd like to go on Sunday because it's a race day."

I said, "I'm not going to stop you. I want you to make your own choices."

He said, "I've been itching to get out there."

I said, "So do it."

He said, "I know I told you I'd never race again."

I was thinking that in the hospital he'd promised not to *ride* again, period. So ride, race, what difference did it make?

That Sunday, he went out. When he came home, I didn't ask him about his day. I never ask because I loathe riding days. About fifteen minutes went by. Finally he said, "Aren't you going to ask how my day was?"

I said, "No, I wasn't going to ask, but how was it?"

He said, "Ask me how the race was."

I said, "How was the race?"

He said, "I got to the track. I paid for the race. But then I thought about how I made a promise in the hospital. I thought of your face and all you've been through, and I didn't do it."

I knew he wanted me to thank him. I couldn't do it. But I said, "I'm proud of you, but I don't want you to do it for me. I want you to do it for the family. Not because I don't want you to, but because you think it's best for the family."

"I thought you'd be happy with my decision."

I said, "Okay, babe, I'm happy, babe, I really am."

The motorcycle thing might always be a bone of contention. He wants to do it, and it will always bother me. At the same time I envy him that feeling of invincibility. How nice it must be not to spend every day living in fear. I've learned that just because something seems right and obvious to me, it doesn't mean that Dean should feel the same way. I can't impose my beliefs on him. This seems so simple in concept, but it's very hard to put into practice. His choice to do something I find insanely dangerous has taken its toll on our relationship. It's done some damage; I won't lie. It will always be part of our history. But I forgive him, we both do our best to listen to each other, and, for the most part, we've moved past it.

I think of me and Dean as a pretty resilient, loving couple. It's always strange to see huge, horrible lies about us in national publications. When *Star* wrote that we were having a three-hundred-million-dollar divorce, it came out of the blue. Three hundred million dollars! I'd divorce him for three million (and remarry him on the spot). This article said that Dean was a sex addict (hence the four kids in six years) and that he'd been plotting to leave me since the beginning. He was going for full custody of the kids—he wanted them for the money.

I'd been around the proverbial *Star* block, but this time something was different. Now Liam could read the headlines. The caption for the divorce article said, "Who will get the kids?" In the checkout line at the grocery store, Liam saw the article and before I could grab it away from him, he read that line out loud to me. "What does it mean? Who's taking us?" he said. The corners of his mouth twitched downward, and I saw his blue eyes filling with tears. I quickly told him it wasn't about him, or us, and flipped the magazine backward on the stand. That night I wrote an open letter to *Star* magazine and posted it on my blog. I wanted these articles to stop, not as a celebrity, but as a mom.

Liam's sixth birthday party was at our house in Westlake Village on a warm Saturday in March. The theme was *Star Wars*. For the first time in my life as a mother, I scaled back. Or tried to. The party was just Liam's classmates. We didn't invite any of our friends except Bill, Scout, and Mehran, all of whom my children know as uncles. Grandma Jacquie and my mom were invited too. But our total number of invitees was twenty. My original list was eighty-five.

When we did parties that were going to air on TV, companies always gave us stuff for free so they could appear on the show. Now, without all those trade-outs, I tried to keep the party affordable. Crocs agreed to sponsor the party. All the young guests would get new Crocs, which would save money on party favors. In exchange, our family would pose for a photo wearing Crocs. I had to stick to a budget for this one. That's right. I said it. Budget.

Even so, now that I was paying attention to every dollar we spent, I saw how costly it was to throw what I would consider a bare-bones party. I mean, I couldn't let go of the dessert table! That's my signature detail! But I scaled back from a six-foot table to a four-foot table.

We got the mini R2-D2 cake, because the twelve-inch one was too expensive. Some of the cake pops were *Star Wars* characters, but most of them were plain ones in the colors of the party because it was more cost-effective. There were Jedi cupcakes and a chalkboard behind it all saying MAY THE FORCE BE WITH YOU. It looked yummy, but it wasn't my normal dessert table.

For the food, we served McDonald's, but we called the chicken fingers "Ewok bites" and the hamburgers "Vader burgers."

Jess and I had hand-sewn Jedi tunics for all the kids to wear. She helped me set up, since I still couldn't lift anything heavy. We were all ready to go half an hour before the party. That had never, ever happened to me before. I always run late and am still setting up when I should be dressing for the party. But this time there was so much less to do that we actually got it all done on time. I couldn't believe it.

Before I got dressed, I surveyed the scene. That oversized house had an oversized front yard. Even with the bouncy house, the face painters, T-shirt-making with *Star Wars* stencils, and the Jedi training station, it looked empty. It was cute, I guess—normal—but it just didn't look like one of my parties.

Fifteen minutes before the party started I was struggling to put Finn into his furry Ewok costume. Liam came running from the jumpy house. "Jack fell," he said. "He fell really hard. There's blood everywhere. He's hurt."

I came running out, and Jack met me in the hall. He had his hands to his face and there was blood pouring out from under them. I'm usually good with blood—I'd certainly seen my share with placenta previa—but I started feeling woozy. Dean was in the kitchen making a veggie option for the party. (I had suggested that he do cheese sandwiches, but Dean is just as bad as I am. He was in the kitchen making tomato-soup shots to go with the grilled cheese.)

I called for Dean, and he came into the hall. As soon as Jack pulled his hands from his face, it wasn't hard to diagnose the injury. He had totally broken his nose. Badly. It curved dramatically to the side. Dean got him into the car and left for the ER. (If anyone knows his way to, around, and home from an ER, it's Dean.)

The hallway looked like a crime scene, and I followed the trail of blood out to the jumpy house. There was a massive amount of blood in it. It looked like someone had killed and drained three large-sized dogs. There were pools of blood, and blood running in rivers down all the seams. My new assistant came over with a bin of wet wipes. I gave him an embarrassed smile. "Welcome aboard?"

During the party, Liam, the birthday boy, was in a mood. He rejected the costumes that he'd wanted everyone to wear. He didn't want to eat anything. He was only persuaded to do a tiny bit of Jedi training. He had to be coerced to cut the cake. He did the piñata under pressure. But all he really wanted to do was to jump, at some points all by himself, in the wiped-down bouncy house. What was I trying to achieve? Who was this party for if not for him? Lesson learned. I should have just had a bouncy house, stuck it in the middle of the yard, and called it a day.

The kicker came when it was time to pose for the photos for Crocs. After we wrangled Liam, which wasn't easy, we posed for a few shots. Dean and Jack weren't there, of course, because they were still at the hospital. Halfway through the pictures Bill leaned in and whispered to me, "You know this is going to be a problem. People are going to notice that Dean's not in any of the photos and they'll say it's because you two are getting divorced."

He was right. As soon as the pictures went online, my publicist started getting calls. It never ends.

I THINK ABOUT the challenges of the past few years—moving houses too many times, falling into debt, the end of *Tori & Dean*, a high-risk pregnancy, and a life-threatening complication—and I can't help but weigh them against the incredible fortune I have. Four healthy babies whom I love more than the world, and a husband who is my confidant, hero, and the love of my life. The more life goes on—the happy and the sad—the closer our family is bound.

I've gained strength and perspective that I wouldn't have had two years ago. I'm coming to terms with who I am—a wife, a mother, Aaron Spelling's daughter. I have dreams I can accomplish, and some that I may have to set aside until the time is right. But I know what is most important to me. My family comes first. I want to make a home for us, one that is simple, and warm, and fabulous (within our means), and somehow fits all of us and our menagerie. I've shown the reality of my life on-screen, and I've shared the reality behind that reality. Now it's time to just live it.

Acknowledgments

I am so grateful for the people in my life, and thankful for everyone who once again helped me share my reality with all of you!

First, the team at Gallery Books, who, among other virtues and publishing geniuses, never complained when I moved around the chickens on the jacket. Many thanks to Jen Bergstrom, Patrick Price, Jennifer Robinson, Kristen Dwyer, Kiele Raymond, and Lisa Litwack.

My fabulous biz peeps who are all dear friends to me . . . Ruthanne Secunda, Gueran Ducoty, Ennis Kamcili, Paula Friedman, Meghan Prophet, Jill Fritzo, Jamie Mandelbaum, Peter Sample, Sara Fernstrom, Dana B., Gary Schneider, Eleanor Burke, Michael Kagan and everyone at

ICM, Dan Strone and Trident, Eqal, Tawil, JCP, Jo-Ann Fabric and Craft Stores, Keeco, and Darice.

And always, my friends and family, who saw me through a revolving hospital door with immense love and unbelievable support: Dean, Jack, Liam, Stella, Hattie, Finn, Mom, Randy (and his beautiful family, Leah, Sage, and Lotus), Mehran, Patsy (and her family), Scout and Bill (aka The Guncles), Simone, Grandma Jacquie, Jenny, Amy, Sara, Jennifer, Marcel, James, Steven, Dr. J, my Canadian family, Aunt Kay, Brandy, Paola, Laura, Randy and Fenton, Jess, Chris W., Seth, Richard, Lindsey, Mo, Megan, Brendan, Anthony, Erica, Mike Rosenthal, Patty Penn, Jill K, Fay, all the amazing doctors, nurses, and staff of Cedar Sinai, and the fabulous Hilary Liftin, who always calls it like it is!

I love you . . .

Tori xoxo